Labor *and* Legality

ISSUES OF GLOBALIZATION
Case Studies in Contemporary Anthropology

Labor and Legality: An Ethnography of a Mexican Immigrant Network
Ruth Gomberg-Muñoz

"Walking Together in the Forest": An Ethnography of Foraging and Farming Women of the Congo Basin
Bonnie Hewlett

Cuban Color in Tourism and La Lucha: An Ethnography of Racial Meanings
L. Kaifa Roland

Labor *and* Legality

An Ethnography of a
Mexican Immigrant Network

Ruth Gomberg-Muñoz
University of Illinois at Chicago

New York   Oxford
OXFORD UNIVERSITY PRESS
2011

Oxford University Press, Inc., publishes works that further Oxford University's
objective of excellence in research, scholarship, and education.

Oxford   New York
Auckland   Cape Town   Dar es Salaam   Hong Kong   Karachi
Kuala Lumpur   Madrid   Melbourne   Mexico City   Nairobi
New Delhi   Shanghai   Taipei   Toronto

With offices in
Argentina   Austria   Brazil   Chile   Czech Republic   France   Greece
Guatemala   Hungary   Italy   Japan   Poland   Portugal   Singapore
South Korea   Switzerland   Thailand   Turkey   Ukraine   Vietnam

Copyright © 2011 by Oxford University Press, Inc.

Published by Oxford University Press, Inc.
198 Madison Avenue, New York, New York 10016
http://www.oup.com

Oxford is a registered trademark of Oxford University Press

Excerpts from some chapters were previously published as follows:
Chapter 2 contains excerpts from Ruth Gomberg-Muñoz (2009), "Not Just Mexico's Problem: Labor
Migration from Mexico to the United States (1900–2000)." *Journal of Latino-Latin American Studies* 3
(3):2–18.
Chapters 1, 5, and 6 contain excerpts from Ruth Gomberg-Muñoz (2010), "Willing to Work: Agency
and Vulnerability in an Undocumented Immigrant Network." *American Anthropologist* 112(2):295–307.

Library of Congress Cataloging-in-Publication Data
Gomberg-Muñoz, Ruth.
Labor and legality : an ethnography of a Mexican immigrant network / Ruth Gomberg-Muñoz.
    p. cm.—(Issues of globalization : case studies in contemporary anthropology)
Includes bibliographical references and index.
ISBN 978-0-19-973938-7
1. Foreign workers, Mexican—Illinois—Chicago—Social conditions.   2. Illegal aliens—Illinois—
Chicago—Social conditions.   3. Mexicans—Illinois—Chicago—Social conditions.   4. Mexico—
Emigration and immigration—Social aspects.   5. United States—Emigration and immigration—
Social aspects.   I. Title.
HD8081.M6G63   2011
331.6′272077311—dc22   2010010845

Printing number: 9 8

Printed in the United States of America
on acid-free paper

CONTENTS

PREFACE

There are few issues in the United States that generate as much interest and controversy as undocumented, or "illegal," immigration. Over the past decade, undocumented immigration has been the centerpiece of national and local political campaigns, news programs, vigilante operations, and mass mobilizations for immigrant rights. In the midst of these highly publicized and deeply polarizing events, some twelve million undocumented people go about their daily lives. This is a story about ten of them.

This book is an attempt to push beyond polarizing rhetoric about "illegal immigrants" and help readers develop a holistic and contextualized understanding of undocumented life. Each chapter opens with a "story," a compilation of interview material from one undocumented worker in his own words. Chapter 1 introduces readers to the Lions, the group of workers who are the focus of this ethnography, and to Il Vino, the restaurant where they work. Chapter 2 considers historical and political contexts of undocumented migration: Why do people move from one place to another? When does the movement of people become "illegal," and why? This review of historical and theoretical literature pertaining to Mexico–U.S. labor migration provides a context for the following chapters, in which the focus shifts to my ethnographic work with the Lions. Chapter 3 explores dimensions of undocumented migration—how people make the decision to migrate, crossing the border, adjusting to life in the United States, and making decisions about whether to settle or return to Mexico. Chapter 4 describes how workers utilize network and household resources to build social bonds and find jobs and living situations; I describe workers' households in detail, including household composition, the distribution of chores and living expenses, and strategies for conflict avoidance. Chapter 5 examines the other central hub of workers' activities: the job site. I show how a cohort of undocumented busboys develops normative behaviors at work that promote a social identity for themselves as "hard workers" with "good attitudes." This social identity, in turn, helps workers cultivate job security and financial stability. Chapter 6 considers the more subjective side of workaday life with a focus on how undocumented immigrants negotiate legal and racial status in ways that promote their dignity and self-esteem. Chapter 6 also explores the broader implications of these workers' behaviors and contradictions, as elements of class society are simultaneously reproduced and resisted in their everyday activities. Finally, Chapter 7 offers a conclusion that considers evidence for some of the widespread beliefs about undocumented migration and argues for an anti-racist, anti-nativist approach to human rights.

Some Notes on Terminology

Throughout this book, I refer to workers who crossed the Mexico–U.S. border without inspection (or government permission) as "undocumented," rather than "illegal." This usage is consistent with recent critical scholarship (e.g. De Genova 2002, 2005; Ngai 2004), as it better reflects the contingent nature of immigration status and avoids the pejorative connotations of "illegal alien" or "illegal immigrant" (see also Chavez 2002; Plascencia 2009). As historian Mae Ngai (2004: xix) notes, "'undocumented' is a historically specific condition that is possible only when documents (most commonly a visa) are required for lawful admission, a requirement that was born under the modern regime of immigration restriction." That is, people are "undocumented" in relation to particular laws in particular places, at particular times in history. Referring to a person as "illegal" glosses the historical and political construction of immigration categories and diminishes the humanity of transmigrant workers. However, the term "undocumented" has its own problems and limitations, and Plascencia (2009) has recently made a compelling case for the more politically sophisticated (if unwieldy) designation "informally authorized migrant."

Scholars can choose from several different words to describe foreign-born people in the United States, including *immigrant, migrant, transmigrant,* and *transborder.*[1] Each term addresses a particular nuance in the relationships of mobile workers to the nation-state, and each has its own merits and drawbacks. I use the term *immigrant* when I describe my ethnographic participants for two related reasons. First, many of them are long-term, if not permanent, settlers in the United States, and *migrant* and *transmigrant* suggest an element of mobility or transience that does not accurately reflect their situations. Second, my research focuses more on workers' daily activities in Chicago and less on their transnational and migration experiences per se. I use *migrant* when referring to those who continually move in the search for work and *transmigrant* when referring to transnationalist scholarship or transnational workers generally.

In chapter 6, I use the term *racialization* to describe the positioning of Mexican workers in relation to the socioeconomic structure of American society. This usage is problematic, as "Mexican" is properly a nationality (though it is also sometimes considered an ethnicity) and is not typically used as a racial classification. Following De Genova and Ramos-Zayas (2003), I use the term "racialization" to draw attention to the process by which, for nonwhites in the United States, ethnicity and nationality are often conflated with race, so that Latin American immigrants in the United States are classified as "Latino" or "Hispanic," regardless of their actual national origin or ethnic identity. Latin Americans in Chicago are frequently labeled "Mexican,"[2] no matter where they are from, converting Mexican into an externally ascribed identity that conflates actual ethnic and national differences—a process of racialization.[3]

The heart of the problem is that all of these categorical terms—race, nationality, ethnicity—are imprecise, frequently conflated, not mutually exclusive, have no fixed set of necessary and sufficient conditions, and fail to capture the complexity of identity. Sociological literature on race and ethnicity recognizes these problems and has tried to clarify usage by, among other things, emphasizing that race tends to be ascribed from without while ethnicity tends to be self-ascribed.[4] That is, there is a degree of flexibility and choice in ethnic identity that is not as characteristic of racial identity.[5]

Acknowledgments

First and foremost, I am grateful to my parents, Paul Gomberg and Mary Conklin Gomberg, who have not only financed most of my rather extended education but have provided unwavering intellectual and emotional support. Many of the central ideas in the book have been developed through conversations with both of my parents, but especially with my father. Most recently, my mother read a draft of this manuscript, and it has benefited enormously from her comments and suggestions.

This book is an elaboration of my doctoral dissertation research, and my dissertation committee deserves special recognition. As committee chair, Alaka Wali shared her expansive anthropological expertise with me and has been instrumental in bringing this project to fruition. John Monaghan was a critical source of support throughout my graduate career and has helped me mature intellectually into a professional anthropologist. Nilda Flores-González has been generous with both her time and her knowledge of immigration and Latinos/as in the United States. Jonathan Haas encouraged me to pursue this project and has shown unfailing support of my research. Joel Palka not only reads everything that I send him but has been extremely helpful with editing and revising.

I am also grateful to Mexican historian Christopher Boyer and sociologist Stephen Steinberg for reading parts of the manuscript and offering valuable criticisms, although I suspect I have not done justice to Dr. Steinberg's arguments. I also appreciate the help of immigration attorney Anel Dominguez, who walked me through some of the intricacies of immigration law.

This material is based upon work supported by the National Science Foundation under Grant No. 0718696. I am indebted to Brian S. Bauer for his patient and unrelenting criticism of my NSF proposal. Mark Liechty also read a draft of the proposal and suggested that I narrow the focus to the agency of undocumented workers—for that, I am very grateful. Francesca Gaiba and Ebony Brooks administered the grant and were instrumental in working out some of the bureaucratic difficulties associated with the project. Of course, any opinions, findings, and conclusions or recommendations expressed in this material are mine alone and do not necessarily reflect the views of the National Science Foundation, or anyone else for that matter.

My colleagues and peers at the University of Illinois–Chicago have formed an academic community that fosters collegial support and intellectual development. I thank Nam C. Kim, Sofia Chacaltana Cortez, Nicola Sharratt, Aleks Markovic, John Michels, Rebecca Deeb, Molly Doane, Betsy Abrams, Crystal Patil, Kathy Rizzo, and Erica Haas-Gallo for their friendship and insights. Special thanks go to Evin Rodkey, Joslyn Hegelmeyer, Laura Nussbaum-Barberena, Jorge Mena, and Stephen Davis, who read parts of this manuscript and offered many valuable comments and suggestions. This book has been written over the course of three years, and various friends have been especially supportive at different points; one in particular, April McCraw Lancaster, deserves special thanks for always being there to put things in perspective.

This book would not have been possible without the support of Janet Beatty and Cory Schneider, the excellent editors at Oxford University Press. I also thank the following reviewers, who put time and care into reading and improving the manuscript: Roberta D. Baer, University of South Florida; Peter Benson, Washington University in St. Louis; Richard Burns, Arkansas State University; Marysia Galbraith, University of Alabama; Mariela Nuñez-Janes, University of North Texas; Adan Quan, Michigan State University; Vicki Root-Wajda, College of DuPage and Elmhurst College; and Jianhua Zhao, University of Louisville.

I would like to thank the workers in and around León, Guanajuato, Mexico, who sacrificed their precious free time to do interviews with me. Special thanks also go to Estela and Shirel, León's best navigators, and Honoria, Jose, Pachita, and Chuy, as well as their families, for their warm hospitality.

Mil gracias [a thousand thank yous] go to my husband, Manuel Muñoz, who has given me unflagging encouragement. He has helped with every aspect of this project's development, from arguing over critical issues, to listening patiently every time I had a new idea, to taking on more than his share of household responsibilities. My love and thanks, Manuel.

Finally, I would like to thank all of the workers who participated in this research. This project is truly a collaborative ethnography because it has been, since its inception, guided and improved by the experiences, observations, and insights of undocumented immigrants that I have known. The cooperation of everyone at Il Vino, including the owners, managers, and staff, has been critical to this project's completion. More than anyone else, the Lions, the ten men who make up the core study participants, have been extremely generous with their time and their ideas. Their support of this research made it possible, and their enthusiastic participation made it come to life. I dedicate this book to them.

Notes

1. See Basch, Schiller, and Blanc 1994; De Genova 2005; Stephen 2007.
2. See also De Genova 2005:271.
3. See also Bashi Bobb 2001; Omi and Winant 1994; Waters 1990.
4. E.g., Nagel 1994; Waters 1990.
5. Nagel 1994.

INTRODUCTION

Like many middle-class students, I worked my way through college, then graduate school, by waiting tables and tending bar. The roots of this project took hold when I was eighteen, taking introductory Spanish classes at the University of Illinois at Chicago, and waiting tables in the evenings. I studied during the day, and when I went to work at night I practiced my rudimentary Spanish vocabulary with the Mexican immigrants who worked in the kitchen and as busboys. Friendships grew from these interactions. Not only did my Spanish improve, but I learned how to eat with tortillas (not well), and I listened as my new friends recounted harrowing stories of their border crossings. The owners and managers at the restaurant disapproved of my friendships with the Mexican workers. They said that it "looked bad" that I talked with the busboys in front of customers since they were "below me." Eventually, the managers told my busboy friends that they would be fired if they did not stop speaking with me while we worked. Shortly after, several of my new friends left the restaurant to return to their hometown in Zacatecas, Mexico, for a visit. I quit and went with them. As I toured their small dusty town, I was struck by its beauty and emptiness, and by the realization that there were no men around— only women, children, and seniors—nearly all of the town's able-bodied men were in the United States. I was profoundly affected by that experience, and when I returned to Chicago, I changed my major to Spanish and began to study Mexican history and culture in earnest.

I first got to know the core participants of this research—a group of friends and co-workers that I call "the Lions"—in 2003. I met them through a mutual acquaintance, and I gradually became friendly with them at

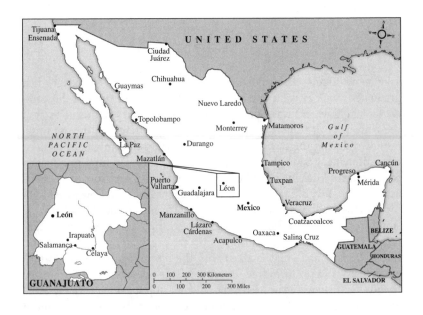

summer barbecues and soccer games. At the time, I had been building friendships with Mexican workers in Chicago for more than a decade and always welcomed the chance to practice my Spanish with new people. Even though I had begun graduate school in anthropology, it did not occur to me to do an ethnography of undocumented workers in Chicago. Instead, I wanted to pursue research that examined how global economic restructuring had changed the activities of people living in peripheral areas. I was particularly interested in "women only" communities in migrant sending regions—an interest that had been provoked by my visit to Zacatecas ten years before. As I became more familiar with the scholarship on migration, and on unauthorized migration in particular, I noticed that there was a dearth of literature that focused on understanding undocumented life from unauthorized workers' points of view. I changed my dissertation topic and, eventually, wrote this book as an attempt to enrich the scholarship on undocumented migration and bolster anthropological theories of how people negotiate everyday problems associated with the demands of global capitalism.

Although this project has been substantially informed by many years of personal interactions with Mexican immigrants in Chicago, the bulk of formal data collection took place between the summer of 2007 and the winter of 2008/2009. During that time I conducted several interviews with each one of the Lions, and I spent time with them at work and at home. In the fall of 2007 and with the owner's permission, I began working at the restaurant where many of them are employed as busboys. Initially, I had also planned to work as a busboy. This plan was quickly abandoned when I realized that the sight of a white woman working as a busboy drew a lot of attention, so instead, I "worked" in other areas of the restaurant: "on the floor" as a waitress and in the kitchen as a food expeditor. Working as a waitress at Il Vino greatly facilitated my ability to do this study, as I could be part of the Lions' workplace interactions without violating the racial and gendered boundaries of the restaurant. I also spent a considerable amount of time as a patron at Il Vino and other restaurants, trying to discern the degree to which the work behaviors that I was observing might be typical. I attended soccer games and birthday parties; I drank beer with the Lions after work and took presents to their families when I went to Mexico. I spent time with the Lions' families in Chicago, as well, and developed friendships with their wives and girlfriends. In addition to the interviews that I conducted with the Lions, I also interviewed five managers at Il Vino, several nonimmigrant co-workers, and two of the Lions' wives.

I also went to Mexico and interviewed the Lions' friends and family members in León, many of whom were returned (and, it turns out, future) migrants themselves. Finally, I interviewed several undocumented Mexican immigrants who also work as busboys but are outside of the Lions' social network, as well as employers of Mexican workers at other establishments. All interviews with immigrant workers were conducted in Spanish expect for those with Alejandro, who prefers English, and all interviews with co-workers and managers were conducted in English. For the sake of protecting participants' privacy, I changed all names and any identifying details, and I omitted some very private information—in particular, I have glossed over discussion of a marital conflict.

By the time the reader reaches the end of this ethnography, he or she will understand that this book presents a somewhat different portrait of undocumented workers than that which is typically presented in popular media. The Lions are neither desperately poor nor particularly lonely. They have as many joyous moments as sorrowful ones. Their lives are not simplistic, and they are neither heroes nor martyrs nor criminals. In the end, my portrayal of the Lions' ups, as well as their downs, does not negate and should not mask the very serious problems and constraints that these workers and millions of other undocumented people face in their daily lives.

CHAPTER ONE

Meet the Lions

A DOG'S LIFE: LUIS

My name is Luis, I am twenty-two years old and I come from León, Mexico. My neighborhood in León is one of most humble places that you can imagine. It's one of the oldest too. The people are humble, working people. When I was a kid, my mind was messed up, you know, from being in the streets and being in trouble. I didn't care about anything then, really, I just tried to have fun. So the things that I was doing, the things that happened to me, I didn't really take them seriously. Actually, I had a lot of problems. I had to go to a rehab for drugs, for inhaling solvents. I was really addicted. You look at me now and I'm chubby, but I was skinny back then, just a string bean.

How have I changed? That's something very special to me, when I left the drug life. I met my wife and I had my sons, and that's basically what got me out of that lifestyle. But when I came to the U.S. I didn't take good care of her. I didn't call her enough or send enough money, and she met someone else, she moved in with another man. And I suffered a lot. To tell the truth, I still love her.

When you come here to the U.S. and you meet someone that is from your state, or even from another state, it doesn't matter, just by living with him you realize that he has the same circumstances as you. The values that your family instilled in you, his family instilled in him too. They are the same values. So people join together because of that, they become friends because of that. I didn't know Chuy before, but when I came here, we met, we hung out together, we became friends, and then we worked together and we've never had any problems. That's because we have the same roots, we have the same values.

A Mexican comes here to work wherever he can find an opportunity. If they offer you a job cleaning shit in the street, you take it. If they give you a job as a dishwasher, you take it. You don't have the chance to do things, like go to school, because you don't get the same opportunities. But I love working at the restaurant, to tell you the truth. I love my job. I mean, there are problems, of course, like anywhere. Sometimes you feel like you're working harder than other people. But if you're among Mexicans, you take care of it, you talk about it, you know.

A Mexican is used to working hard. So, I think that an American is not worth as much as a Mexican; he doesn't work the same as a Mexican. It's like I told you: a Mexican takes risks, and an American— if he sees that something is difficult or a job is dangerous—he won't do it. So I think that the boss would rather have a worker who dares to do things, who has enough courage to do the job. I think that's why the boss would rather hire illegals than Americans.

Five words that describe me? Ha ha. Well, first, friendly. Second, I know how to get along with people. Another thing could be, I don't know, that I have a good heart; you know, I don't talk bad about people unless they do something to me. I have a really good heart that I got from my Mom. I don't know, I'm nice, happy, you know. That's how I would describe myself: happy, lively, and ready to work. Maybe a little crazy. A cheerful guy. That's it.

For me, the most important thing in life is my family. Since I was a little kid, my mom taught me that. And so that's the most important thing for me, family, and then health and work. Maybe another thing is to have a conscience, like be a good person so that people know you as a good person and not because you're a drug addict or because you drink too much. But like I said, the most important things are family and health. Money is nothing. It's necessary but it doesn't buy you a good life.

Yes, I think about being illegal. Because if you come here illegally and you have a family and you have kids, you could still get deported. So because of that, you can't aspire to anything; you come here with the mentality to improve yourself and move forward, but what can I do? If I get married, have a family, they could send me back to my country. Mentally, it affects you because you're always thinking that you're a wetback. It's psychological, it's in your head all the time. If you're calm, if you keep your head, you can get along okay, but you always carry that fear with you.

What are my plans for the future? Oooh, well, I have a dog's life. I have always had problems, with drugs, with gangs, I lost my family. You know what I mean? My future, I want to have a future, I don't know what yet, but I want to do something to help my kids so they're proud of me. But you know, one makes plans and then things fall apart. But if God gives me the chance, I see myself living with my kids in a little house.

I WANT RESPECT AT MY JOB: RENE

My name is Rene and out of all these guys, I'm the best one. No, I'm just kidding! Seriously, I was fifteen when I first came to the United States. I had been studying to be an electrician in Mexico, but I left the year before I graduated. I wanted to come here to do something different, to improve myself. I was at that age when you think you can do anything in the world.

I got the job at Il Vino because the owner knew me from the previous restaurant I worked at. So I started working there and at first I was just a regular busboy but then they saw that I worked my ass off and they promoted me to head busboy. But I never felt like the boss of anybody. And when the managers would tell me, "Hey, tell that guy to come clean this," I would never tell him, "Hey, do this because the boss says so." I would just go clean it myself. I prefer to do it myself and that way I know there won't be any problems.

When they promoted me they gave me a raise, and every couple of months they gave me commission. They have always given me commission. Like if it was a really busy Saturday night, sometimes Tony would tell me, "Here, take five-hundred bucks." Just for one night. He'd tell me, "Thanks, everything went really well tonight." When I got back from my honeymoon, they gave me money. They asked me, "How much did you spend on your honeymoon?" "Oh, like two or three thousand." And two hours later they came back and gave me an envelope with all the money I had spent. I didn't expect them to do that, I never thought they would do that. And when there was a lot of work and they were happy they would give me two-hundred, three-hundred, five-hundred dollars.

I'm not afraid of losing my job, right, because I like to work, I know that I will find another job. But I wouldn't want to lose my job for being lazy. I want them to respect me. You know that there are like ten managers at Il Vino and I don't want them to tell me what to do. And so that's why I work so hard, so that none of them has any-thing to say to me. Maybe if I were to take a break, they would come and tell me, "Do this, do that, do this," and if I don't do it, they're going to send me home. And I won't have respect. I prefer to always work, so no one will say anything to me.

I've had lots of bosses and they've all treated me the same, I've never had a bad boss. And I've seen them get angry even with a Latino, because the boss treats you according to how you work for him. If you're not a good worker, he's going to be following you, criticizing you, "Do this, work harder." If you work hard for him, he won't bother you. As long as you're making him money, the boss is always going to be happy with you. I think that's why they say you can win the boss over. Don't always wait around for work to do, right, like if your section isn't busy, go to the kitchen, run food or whatever, you know? And they are always noticing who works and who doesn't work. And when you win them over, they don't watch you anymore, they give you—you win their respect.

I don't work hard to kiss ass. I don't want to be like, "Look boss, let me clean your shoes, let me do this," you know? I just go to work, do my job, go home. American workers are like, "How are you boss? A chair, boss? A soda, boss?" I don't talk to Tony much, just about work. But I don't have my job from kissing the bosses' ass. They like the way I work and that's why they keep me. That's why I don't walk around kissing ass. I want respect at my job.

I would like to get a professional job one day. For me a profes-sional job would be a job with the union. They give you benefits and send you to school. You know that with a restaurant job, if you don't have a good job in the restaurant, sometimes you only make three-hundred, three-hundred fifty dollars a week. But if you have papers you could get a job that teaches you a lot and helps you out a lot more. And then, if I don't work nights anymore, I could be with my kids in the evenings.

Despite differences in their pasts and divergent prospects for the future, Luis and Rene have many things in common. They were born in differ-ent neighborhoods of the same city—León, Guanajuato, Mexico—and are part of the same transnational network that moves between León and Chicago, Illinois. (See the map at the beginning of the text.) Here in the U.S., they share the stigma of being "illegal aliens" and the dignity of being hard workers and family men. As undocumented immigrants, Luis and Rene face serious constraints on their everyday choices and actions, yet both are engaged in a workaday struggle to improve their lives in spite of those constraints. They are two among millions of such people who live and work in the United States without legal authorization.

At its broadest level, this book explores how "Men make their own history, but not of their own free will."[1] It begins with the premise that undocumented immigrants develop strategies to enhance their well-being as workers in the United States. Two parallel arguments are developed throughout. The first is that illegal status poses specific challenges to undocumented people, circumscribing their opportunities and affecting their everyday activities; the second argument is that undocumented workers alter their prospects—alter their circumscription, in fact—through their agency. This is not a story about victimization, but an examination of the daily struggles that workers wage to make their lives better.

An understanding of the ways in which illegal status constrains people's life situations is central to this analysis. But the focus of this book is not constraint per se; it is people and their effective, purposeful activities–their human agency. When the concept of agency is applied to undocumented immigrants, the question arises as to whether these workers are actually exercising agency or are merely doing what they have to in order to survive. This latter interpretation suggests that the highly controlled environment in which undocumented immigrants live and work largely deprives them of meaningful choice and agency. But while human agency represents power in a broad sense of capability for action, it is not reducible to empowerment. Rather, agency is the human capacity to exert some control over the conditions of one's existence. Inequality differentially constrains the scope and effectiveness of agency, such that this small group of undocumented workers is unlikely to impact U.S. immigration policy or even change their subordinate status at the restaurants where they work. Nevertheless, as I will show, they can and do effectively shape their lives through their collective agency.[2]

The primary academic contribution of this project resides in its "thick description" of the workaday agency of intensely marginalized people. In particular, an attention to the activities of undocumented immigrants contributes to existing literature on globalization and migration that has tended to focus on the global processes that generate migration and funnel workers into low-wage jobs with little security.[3] By shifting the focus to workers' agency, this research complements those analyses and shows how undocumented immigrants navigate the terrain of work and society in the United States. More broadly, as it examines how inequalities are perpetuated and resisted in the everyday activities of marginalized workers, this study contributes, if only modestly, to anthropological theories of social reproduction and change. Finally, a focus on the everyday lived realities of undocumented people pushes past one-dimensional stereotypes of "illegal immigrants" as mere victims or criminal usurpers, and emphasizes their complex humanity.[4]

Meet the Lions

This is an ethnography of a cohort of ten undocumented men—Alberto, Alejandro, Chuy, Lalo, Leonardo, Luis, Manuel, Omar, Rene, and Roberto. These men live in the Chicago area and work as busboys in suburban Chicago restaurants. They are young workers, in their early twenties to mid-thirties, who are all undocumented though four of them have wives and/or children who are U.S. citizens. These workers are close friends, and in some cases brothers and cousins, who substantially share their work and social lives with each other. Although they work as many as sixty hours a week, they make time to get together every Wednesday in the summer to play soccer, and Sundays are good days for impromptu get-togethers with ample Mexican food and beer.

These workers playfully refer to themselves as "mojarones." "Mojarón" is derived from "mojado," which means "wet," but in this context is slang for "wetback," the pejorative term for Mexican immigrants popular in the United States for much of the twentieth century. I considered using "mojarón" as a shorthand term for the core participants of this project for several reasons. First and most importantly, it is how they refer to themselves. Second, "mojarón" alludes to the legal, racial, and class status of the group, as well as to the agency of the workers in engaging that status. After consideration, however, I could not bring myself to use a term derived from a racial slur. Instead, I call them "the Lions" for short, a nod to León ("Lion"), Mexico, their city of origin.

All of the Lions are real people (not composites), and I have truthfully described their personalities, histories, and activities.[5] In order to help protect their anonymity, I have changed all names, nicknames, any details that could identify them (such as physical characteristics or details of events), and, in some cases, the particulars surrounding how I came to know them. We all hope—the Lions and I—that changes in immigration legislation will allow them to "come out of the closet" and will enable me to discuss in complete frankness the circumstances of our interactions.

While I have tried to capture the scale, pace, economy, and culture of the real-life restaurants where the Lions work, the description of "Il Vino Buono" is a fictitious composite of several restaurants that I have spent time in, as is "Uncle Luigi's" and any other establishment I name herein. While there are many large-scale restaurants in the Chicago area

The Lions

Name	Age	Work Situation	Family Status	Household Arrangement
Alberto "Dumbo"	32	Il Vino busboy	wife and three children in Mexico	lives with his brothers Alejandro and Carlos and his brother-in-law Luis in a rented house
Alejandro "Buddha"	35	former Uncle Luigi's busboy; currently manager at uncle's restaurant	divorced, citizen son lives in Chicago	lives with his brothers Alberto and Carlos and Alberto's brother-in-law Luis in a rented house
Chuy "Lunchbox"	31	Il Vino busboy	single	lives with Rene, his brother
Lalo "el Don"	36	Il Vino busboy	wife and two sons in Mexico; one son in Chicago	lives with sister-in-law and her family
Leonardo "Abercrombie"	24	Il Vino busboy	single	lives with Roberto and two others in an apartment
Luis "el Coco Loco"	22	Il Vino busboy	divorced, two sons in Mexico	lives with his brother-in-law Alberto and Alberto's two brothers

Continued

The Lions *Continued*

Name	Age	Work Situation	Family Status	Household Arrangement
Manuel "Panzon"	30	former Il Vino busboy, currently works side jobs in construction	citizen wife and three children in Chicago	lives with family at wife's parents' house
Omar "el Bravo"	27	Uncle Luigi's cook	citizen wife and child in Chicago	lives with family at wife's parents' house
Rene "Cejón"	29	Il Vino busboy	citizen wife and two children in Chicago	lives with family and Chuy in a house he and his wife own
Roberto "el Flower"	28	Il Vino busboy	single	lives with Leonardo and two others in an apartment

that could easily fit Il Vino's description, all of its details—including the type of cuisine, floor-plan, décor, and characteristics of the owners and managers—are my invention.

Alberto is the shy one. He is thirty-two years old and is also known as "Dumbo," (pronounced Doombo) in reference to the cartoon elephant, because his friends say his ears are too big for his head. Of all the busboys, Alberto is the most quiet and is more often the good-natured target of practical jokes than the instigator. He is very well mannered, smiling a lot and going out of his way to greet everyone at work. He misses his wife and three daughters, who are in Mexico. His goal is to make enough money this time in the U.S. (his third) so that when he goes back to Mexico he won't ever have to return. Alberto lives with his older brother Alejandro, his brother-in-law Luis and his younger brother Carlos—all of whom have worked as Il Vino busboys.

Alejandro has been in the U.S. the longest—nearly twenty years. At thirty-five years old, Alejandro is one of the oldest and presumably wisest of the cohort and has earned the nickname "Buddha" from his friends. Alejandro was married to a white U.S. citizen, but they have since divorced. He has a son by that marriage, Alejandro Jr., or "A.J.," who often accompanies Alejandro to the park for soccer games or to Rene's house for barbecues. Alejandro lives with Alberto, Luis, and Carlos in a small but neat house that they rent in a quiet Chicago suburb. He has worked in restaurants since he came to the U.S. and has been a busboy, busboy manager, and—unique among his friends—a waiter in that time. While Alejandro is a regular at Wednesday night soccer games, he is most often in the company of his girlfriend, a young white waitress that he met at his uncle's restaurant.

Chuy is the rebel. He is Rene's older brother and matches his brother's energy at work and on the soccer field. He is shy until you get to know him, then he shows off a wicked sense of humor. His friends call Chuy "Lunchbox," because they say he can stash food in his square jaw to eat later. Of all the busboys, Chuy is the most politicized and the most sensitive to perceived discrimination at work. He is quick to anger, and this gets him into occasional trouble at Il Vino, though he is also regarded as a very good worker. Chuy rents a small apartment on the second floor of Rene's house and enjoys playing with his dog and working on his rusty 1987 Camaro in his spare time.

Lalo is the "old man." A lifetime of hard work is revealed by Lalo's wrinkles and, according to him, his gray hair; he seems older than his thirty-six years. As the oldest of the group, he endures the constant ribbing from his younger coworkers with a good sense of humor. The guys call Lalo "el Don," or "Sir," in a teasing show of respect for his age. In spite of the teasing, the busboys at Il Vino like and respect Lalo and have defended him to the managers (who perceive him as slow) on more than one occasion.

Leonardo is the fashion plate. The guys sometimes call him "Abercrombie" because he is often dressed head-to-toe in the trendy brand Abercrombie & Fitch, down to the preppy boxers that peek above his fashionably baggy pants. Leonardo is young, outgoing, and confident, which gains him lots of friends and also the occasional accusation of arrogance. He lives with Roberto and two other Mexican immigrants in a two-bedroom apartment in Chicago's suburbs. Leonardo considers himself serious and goal-oriented, though he is the one of the youngest Lions at twenty-four years old.

Luis carries the weight of the world on his shoulders. Abused by his father in Mexico, he became addicted to inhalants at the tender age of ten and has battled drug addiction ever since. His problems worsened when he came to Chicago to be with his brother Omar, since he says drugs and gangs are "on every corner" in his south suburban neighborhood. Since he began working at Il Vino, he has been trying to go straight and get his life together. In spite of his troubles, Luis is generous and laughs easily, but he worries about his future. The busboys call Luis "Coco," which is short for "El Coco Loco," ("the crazy brain"), because of his forays into drugs and crime. At twenty-two years old, he is the youngest of the bunch and enjoys playing Xbox with his brother-in-law Carlos and hanging out with his many friends.

Manuel is a family man. Like Alejandro, he has been in the U.S. for a long time and has established his home and family here. When he's not at work, thirty-year-old Manuel is usually accompanied by his troupe of three sons and his young wife Liliana. Manuel worked as a busboy for many years but is also an experienced carpenter; he can often be found helping his friends with various home improvement projects. Manuel is always laughing and is fun to be around, even though he recently lost his construction job and has been battling unemployment ever since. The guys call Manuel "Panzón" or "Fatty" because of his ever-growing middle.

Omar "el Bravo" is small and energetic, much like the soccer star he is nicknamed after. Like Alejandro and Manuel, he has been in the United States for more than a decade and will likely never go back to Mexico to live. He is married to a white American citizen who also happens to be the daughter of his employer—a situation that has caused no small amount of controversy at the restaurant where he works. Omar has forged an uneasy alliance with his American family and is the proud father of a new baby girl. Omar also looks after his younger brother Luis and does his best to keep him out of trouble.

Rene is the role model. He is quiet but friendly, always energetic, and, of all the busboys, he is the most esteemed by the management of Il Vino. Although he is often made the de-facto head busboy, Rene rejects being in a position of authority and prefers to work cooperatively with the other guys. His friends have nicknamed Rene "Cejón," or "Unibrow," because they say he has one long, continuous, bushy eyebrow. He is always busy, at home and at work, and can be counted on to help a friend at any time. He owns a home with his Irish-American wife Molly and has two young children that he enjoys taking on excursions around the city of Chicago.

Roberto is the cute one. He is the frequent object of flirtatious glances from waitresses and female customers alike. To widespread disappointment, he is in a serious relationship with a young teacher who also manages at the restaurant where Roberto worked before he came to Il Vino. Roberto is twenty-eight and is well-respected by the other busboys because he is a hard worker and is always willing to help out. He is very friendly and fancies himself something of a soccer star. When Roberto is not at work, he can often be found jogging or lifting weights at the neighborhood gym. The other guys call Roberto "el Flower," because he is so pretty.

Il Vino Buono

"Il Vino Buono," or "The Good Wine,"—hereafter "Il Vino"—is an Italian-villa-themed restaurant that features a dining room with seating for up to three hundred diners, a large lounge/bar area, an outside patio, two banquet rooms, catering, and live music on weekends. It is an enormous place, nearly 25,000 square feet, that is always bustling with a staff of over one hundred people, from dishwashers to decorators and valet drivers to managers. The weekends are always very busy at Il Vino; guests can wait up to an hour or more before they are seated. The lounge fills up quickly, and the bar sells thousands of dollars in wine alone on Friday and Saturday. Sunday through Thursday are less busy, but daily specials like two-for-one bottles of wine and half-price entrées keep a steady crowd coming through the doors.

Il Vino was opened by a husband and wife, Tony and Colleen, eleven years ago. Tony is the son of Italian immigrants and spent his younger years working in the steel mills before getting into the restaurant business. With their investments from other restaurants, the couple built Il Vino from the ground up. It is an impressive stucco building, styled like an ornate Italian villa with lots of wood beams, high ceilings, and an enormous fireplace in the center of the main dining room. This is upscale Italian dining that features fresh seafood, thick steaks, and expensive wines. The building's location in a suburban mall parking lot does little to dampen the high-end atmosphere. (See Figure 1.1.)

As is typical in restaurants, the staff at Il Vino is strictly segregated.[6] The front-of-the-house staff, which includes managers, hosts, servers, and bartenders, is nearly all white. The back-of-the-house staff, which includes busboys, dishwashers, and line cooks, is all Mexican immigrant. The night-shift busboys, who are also Lions, are the most highly paid and, arguably, have the most esteemed job of all the Mexican immigrant workers at Il Vino.

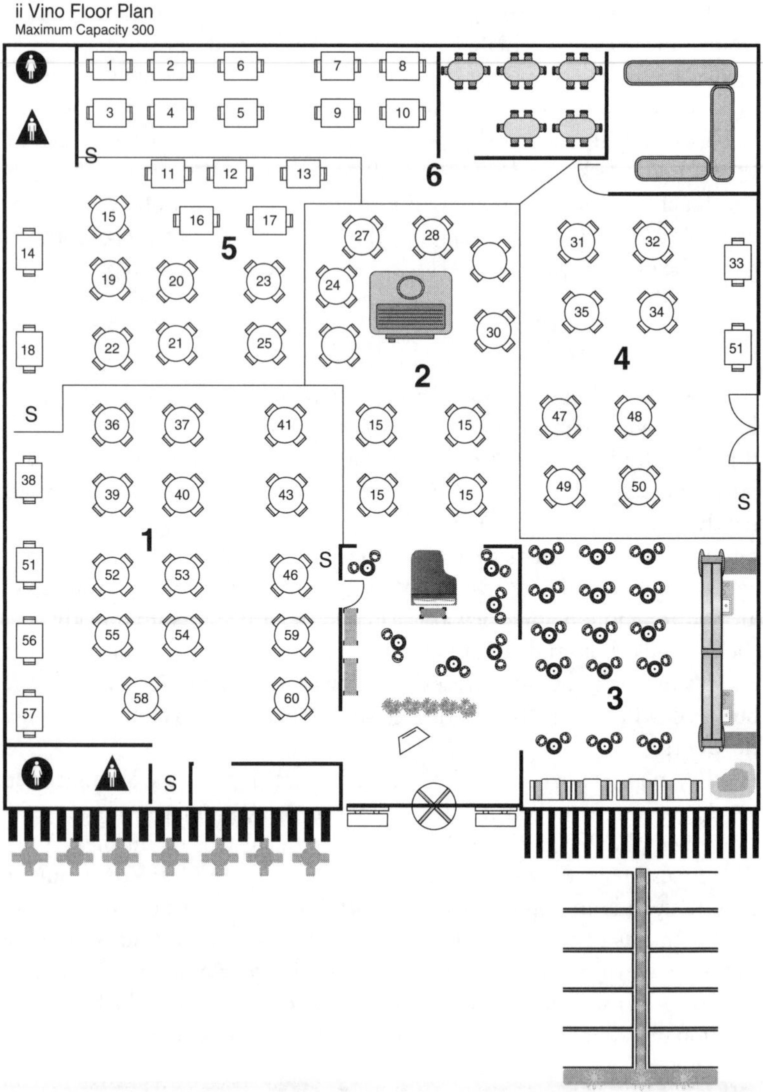

ii Vino Floor Plan
Maximum Capacity 300

FIGURE **1.1 Hypothetical floor plan of "Il Vino;" busboy sections are numbered and "S" represents the location of server stations.** (*Courtesy of the author*)

What Does a Busboy Do?

A busboy can be narrowly defined as support service staff whose duties include clearing tables of dirty dishes, serving water and bread, helping servers carry food trays, putting leftovers in to-go containers, and "turning over" tables when diners leave (removing dirty linens, dishes, and silverware, and replacing them with clean ones). Busboys are typically responsible for their own sections. Sections can vary in size, but at Il Vino each busboy section is usually comprised of three smaller sections that each have one server and five four-person tables (which can be pushed together to accommodate larger parties). In other words, on an average night, a busboy is supporting three servers, fifteen tables, and sixty diners at once. When attending to his section, it is imperative that a busboy be quick, attentive, and helpful.

For reasons that I explore later, the busboys at Il Vino take care of their sections and do much, much more. Nightly, in addition to bussing tables, the busboys sweep and mop the restaurant, clean the bathrooms (there are two each for men and women), empty the garbage cans, wipe down all tables and chairs, set all of the tables, stock the server stations with water glasses, dishes, napkins, straws, and silverware, stock the front bar with beer, liquor, and glassware, and set up banquet rooms for any parties. Since it is nearly impossible to accomplish all of this while being attentive to their sections, the busboys often do not finish their work until two to three hours after Il Vino has closed for the evening. During the day shift, busboys dust, clean windows, and fix whatever needs fixing, as well as bus their sections.

In addition to bussing, cleaning, and setting up, which are considered the busboys' "regular" duties, busboys are responsible for performing any task that falls outside of the other employees' job descriptions. Busboys unclog toilets, clean martini-induced vomit, change customers' flat tires, trap mice, organize storage rooms, move furniture, paint, salt the parking lot when it snows, water the plants, and scrape gum from the bottom of tables. In a pinch, they can also be counted on to cook, bartend, and perform minor first aid.

While busboy is an unskilled job that doesn't require advanced education or training, it is not easy, particularly in a high-end, high-volume restaurant like Il Vino. A good busboy will understand how to time a multiple-course meal (i.e., when to clear appetizer plates so that soup and salad can be served), will anticipate the needs of guests and servers, will be able to socialize appropriately with guests, and will be composed while working for prolonged periods under intense pressure. He must be very fast, very efficient, and very capable. It often takes several years of experience before a worker earns his coworkers' respect as a capable and talented bus-boy. It is the busboys' competence and flexibility, along with the appar-ent enthusiasm and diligence with which they work, that has earned them very high regard from coworkers and managers and has solidified their reputation as "the best workers we have at Il Vino."

While busboys work very hard doing a job that is somewhat socially degraded, many young men apply for busboy positions at Il Vino and are not hired. The busboys say that they like their jobs most of the time, and the highest paid busboys have annual incomes that near the U.S. national average. The owners at Il Vino do not save money, at least not directly, by hiring undocumented immigrants: the Mexican workers are paid the minimum wage, the same as the occasional nonimmigrant busboy, though much of their income is earned as cash tips. In all, these undocumented Mexican immigrants hold jobs that, relative to many other opportuni-ties available to unskilled working-class men, offer them a degree of both social interaction and living wages.

How Do the Lions Compare to Other Groups of Workers?

Undocumented Mexican workers in the United States experience a range of work opportunities, financial conditions, living situations, and degrees of social interaction and exclusion. Leo Chavez (1992:2) explains that there is a "continuum of experience" among undocumented immigrants in the U.S. The immigrants featured in Chavez's 1992 book *Shadowed Lives*, who sleep in irrigation ditches or in makeshift camps that they erect on the San Diego hills, represent one end of this continuum. The Lions fall toward the higher end of the continuum in terms of their income and standard of living. While the average wage of undocumented workers is just over the minimum wage, as many as one in three undocumented males in Chicago earns over ten dollars an hour;[7] nationally, many undocumented workers earn upwards of fifteen and even twenty dollars an hour.[8] The Lions earn annual incomes between twenty-five thousand and thirty-five thousand dollars, including their wages and tips, or roughly between ten and fifteen dollars an hour. They are not poor, and many even have a little wealth in the form of real estate in Mexico, but while being a busboy offers quick cash—and sometimes lots of it—there is no job security. The Lions do not have the independence of the self-employed or the financial stability of the wealthy; moreover, the money that they earn is diffused throughout their families in the U.S. and in Mexico, making it difficult to establish long-term economic security and leaving them dependent on regular full-time employment.

The Lions are considered "the best workers that we have" by their supervisors and coworkers alike, an association of Mexican immigrants with hard work that is not unique to Il Vino. The notion that undocumented Mexican immigrants are superior low-wage workers has wide popular currency and has been noted in several studies.[9] This putative superiority tends to be popularly framed in terms of Mexican workers' "culture" or race. I explore ideas about culture and race more in Chapters 5 and 6, but these studies and my own research suggest that the Lions' reputations as hard workers—and the behaviors that give rise to them—are not unusual among Mexican immigrants in the United States.

Although social inclusion/exclusion is difficult to measure, the Lions appear typical insofar as they are embedded in social networks with fellow Mexican immigrants, but are somewhat atypical in that they regularly interact socially with nonimmigrant, non-Latino Americans. A host of conditions—including an immigrant-friendly atmosphere at Il Vino, the youth, style, and urban origins of the Lions, and the social nature of service/hospitality work—has probably facilitated the development of interracial friendships and romances for the Lions. In fact, of the five unmarried Lions, four—Alejandro, Chuy, Leonardo, and Roberto—are dating non-immigrant white women, and Rene and Omar are married to white women. Such a high degree of social integration with nonimmigrant "whites" is probably somewhat unusual among undocumented Mexican immigrants.

Overall, the Lions represent a relatively successful group of undocumented Mexican workers insofar as their income and social esteem is probably slightly higher than the average for all undocumented Mexican workers.[10] However, the Lions are still fairly typical on all counts, with the possible exception of degree of social integration with white Americans. The Lions' relative success combined with their overall typicality make them ideal participants of a research project that is concerned with how undocumented workers develop strategies to maximize their well-being as their choices are constrained by class, race, and legal status.

The Lions are a highly homogeneous and related group who cultivate some strategies and behaviors and not others. There are, of course, other groups of workers—including undocumented Mexican workers—who cultivate different strategies and behaviors to cope with similar life situations. While the purpose of this ethnography is to provide a micro-level look at one group of workers, and not to present a comparison of different groups of workers, I do try to address variation and alternatives whenever I can. The Lions are very aware of these alternatives and often defend their own behaviors by comparing them to other choices. When workers who adopt different strategies work together, this can generate conflict, and I discuss this as well.

Of course, it should also be stressed that neither the strategies and behaviors, nor the risks and challenges discussed here are limited to undocumented workers. Undocumented Mexican workers are intensely marginalized, but many of the conditions that they experience—lack of economic opportunities, discrimination, poverty, hardship—are shared by countless U.S. citizens. This ethnography took place just outside of the city of Chicago; about half of Chicago Public High School students do not graduate and will likely face extremely limited opportunities in a post-industrial job market. Many young people who are native to the country and citizens with full rights also grapple with financial insecurity, family responsibilities, and criminalization and racism. Many of them probably develop strategies to deal with these obstacles that are very similar to those that the Lions develop.

Nevertheless, the experiences of Mexican immigrants in the U.S. are uniquely shaped by Mexico's particular history and its relationship with the United States. Understanding the life situations of the Lions—why they decide to come to the U.S. and what they do once they get here—requires understanding the broader political and economic context of their lives. This broader context is the subject of the next chapter.

Notes

1. Marx 1973 [1852]: 146.
2. This is a simple conception of structure, culture, and agency that will undoubtedly fail to satisfy some scholars who are concerned with more nuanced considerations of each term. For more developed theoretical discussions of the interaction of structure, culture, and agency, see Giddens 1993, Gunewardena and Kingsolver 2007, Ortner 2006, and Sewell 1992.
3. E.g., Heyman 1998; Kearney 2004; Massey et al. 1994, Massey, Durand, and Malone 2002; Ngai 2004; Portes and Walton 1981; Sassen 1988; but see Chavez 1992; Zlolniski 2006.
4. There are several existing excellent and humanizing ethnographic accounts of the lives of Mexican immigrants in the United States, many of whom are undocumented. In particular, works by Chavez (1992), Conover (1987), De Genova (2005), and Zlolniski (2006) have been especially influential in shaping this study.
5. For the purposes of clarity and organization, I describe the Lions' family and living situations as they were when I officially began research in the summer of 2007. While this strategy is designed help prevent confusion for the reader, it may also give the false impression that the Lions' lives are static

and unchanging. For a description of how the Lions' lives have changed since the initiation of the research project, please see the Epilogue.

6. See also Adler 2005; Fine 1996; Pribilsky 2007.

7. Mehta et al. 2002.

8. Kochhar 2005.

9. E.g., De Genova 2005; Moss and Tilly 2001; Neckerman and Kirschenman 1991; Waldinger and Lichter 2003.

10. See Mehta et al. 2002.

CHAPTER TWO

Why Is There Undocumented Migration?

PAPA JUAN'S STORY

I was born in 1921, on the last day of August. August 31st. I was born right here, right in this town. My father worked on this land parcel [*ejido*], and since I was a little boy I worked on the land too. We grew wheat, garbanzo beans, white corn, sorghum, and alfalfa. I still have eight hectares of land. I don't work them anymore, I'm too old, but I sharecrop them out. Right now, I'm growing alfalfa, masa, and white corn. We have always been people who work this local land [*ejidatarios*].

I first heard about the braceros during the war in 1942. I didn't go [to the U.S. then] because the word was that they would send you to fight in the war, to replace the soldiers who had died. So two of my friends went and they invited me, but I didn't go. I was happy here, working with my animals.

The first time I went to the U.S. was in 1949, but that time I went undercover [without papers]. That was my first adventure. We entered in Mexicali and we walked to Calexico. There, I picked lettuce and washed dishes and watered alfalfa. In the morning, lettuce, then I would wash the dishes, then water the alfalfa at night. How much do you think they paid me an hour? Forty cents. And the American workers were making fifty cents. So one day I said to the boss, "Forty cents an hour seems like very little to me, so if you need someone, I'd like to work where I can make a little more money." And so he found me work watering alfalfa, but that was at night. And they paid me fifty cents an hour for that.

The first time that I worked as a bracero, I went to Arkansas to pick cotton. That was in 1951. I went to Arkansas, cotton; I went to Harlingen [Texas], cotton; I went to Raymondville [Texas], cotton. Each of those times, I entered at Reynosa, and it was pure cotton. When I went to the San Joaquin Valley in California, I finally changed jobs. There, they put me to work picking tomatoes. The last time that I went there to work was in 1962. After that, I had too much work to do here and I couldn't leave.

In those days, I was really strong and I could lift and carry the sacks of cotton. I had to carry a sack that was about six feet long. In Arkansas, picking cotton paid three cents a pound. But there were times when they cheated you and paid you [for] less than you had. There was one time that I had one-hundred and fifty pounds and they barely paid me for one hundred of them. Also, they only gave you permission to stay for forty-five days. What can a person do in forty-five days? During the war, they would give you as much as six months and the chance to renew your permit. Then later on, just forty-five days. You can't make anything in forty-five days.

There were times that we would work all week—even on Sundays. Sundays were supposed to be our day off, so we could put our affairs in order and everything, but sometimes local white farmers would come and bring us corn on the cob [elote] and we would go work with them, picking cauliflower. They gave us rubber suits to wear so that we wouldn't get wet, but they were too hot; we couldn't tolerate them. The sun would touch you, and it was like being hugged in hot rubber. But, anyway, the bracero permit was only for weekdays, and so when farmers would come on Sunday looking for workers, that was extra money for us.

Did I invest the money that I made in my farm? No, there was barely enough money to take care of the family. And in Harlingen they would take almost all the money that you had made at the customs office. There was once, when I was courting my wife, that I bought some fabric for her dresses. And I bought myself some bibbed pants, and I wrapped the fabric around my waist like a belt so they wouldn't take it. Ha ha. And they never saw it.

How many grandchildren do I have in the United States? [Turns to ask his daughter, who counts them: *Well, Chela has five children, Maria has two, Miguel has two, Luci has one, Josefa has two....*] I have about twenty grandchildren there. In all, I have about fifty grandchildren and twenty great-grandchildren. My family could start a town all by itself!

Papa Juan sits comfortably in the shade of his patio, examining hands that are gnarled from seven decades of farm work and nearly that many years of fast-pitch baseball. His wife, Mama Lina, is with him, as are three of his eleven adult children, innumerable giggling grandchildren, and a new puppy. As the women talk, Papa Juan stands up and makes his way over to the pen that houses his few remaining cows. He throws some hay over the wooden fence, then walks past his son Ramón's house toward the alfalfa field. This is the land that Papa Juan inherited as a small child, his parcel of land guaranteed to each landless man by concessions made at the end of the Mexican Revolution (1910–1917). Papa Juan's land is about thirty miles outside of the city of León, Guanajuato; he has worked it his whole life, and now three of his sons work it too. (See Figures 2.1 and 2.2.)

The connection between Papa Juan's family and the United States did not end with his time as a bracero. On the contrary, four of Papa Juan's adult children are now legal permanent residents of the United States; their children—his grandchildren—are U.S. citizens. Because of these relations and Papa Juan's time as a bracero, he and Mama Lina have visas that allow them to visit the United States whenever they want. This makes Papa Juan and Mama Lina the only members of the family in Mexico who have regular physical contact with Rene and Chuy, the only sons of Papa Juan's oldest daughter Maria and undocumented immigrants living in Chicago.

FIGURE 2.1 **Papa Juan at home tending to his animals.** (*Courtesy of the author*)

FIGURE 2.2   Papa Juan's son Ramón built this house outside of León with the money he earned working in agriculture and landscaping in California; Ramón is now a legal permanent resident of the United States. (*Courtesy of the author*)

I conducted this interview with Papa Juan in the spring of 2008, amidst heated political debates in the United States concerning immigration policy. As I toured Papa Juan's small town, I learned that I had just missed labor recruiters who frequent the area. These recruiters are hired by U.S. businesses to enlist Mexican workers to come and fill jobs in their companies; in exchange, the businesses sponsor the Mexican workers' temporary work visas. I was surprised to hear that labor recruiters still come to Papa Juan's town looking for workers, since this was a time of widespread resentment over the number of immigrants already in the United States. Why would U.S. businesses still be recruiting workers from Mexico? And why would Mexican workers leave the comforts of their homes and families to work for low wages in a strange land, subjecting themselves to this resentment? The answers to these questions are complex, but understanding the conditions that have given rise to an interdependence between Mexican workers and U.S. businesses is crucial to understanding how men like the Lions come to live and work in the United States without legal authorization.

Over the past ten millennia, the development of agricultural production and the subsequent rise of state societies has generated mass migrations to population centers. More recently, a particular kind of migration that involves people moving from one place to another in search of paid work, or labor migration, has become increasingly important. Labor migration is tied to the spread of economic practices that make it difficult for people to continue to make their living in some areas—"economic peripheries"—while they create demand for workers in centers of production. International labor migration occurs when these economic practices cross national boundaries. *Undocumented* or illegal migration has become salient as a result of the fortification of national borders that restricts the movement of workers but not jobs, goods, or money—in effect, when policies simultaneously stimulate and "illegalize" international migrant labor.[1] Current large-scale movement of workers from Mexico to the United States is this kind of migration.

A History of Mexican Labor Migration to the United States

The Beginnings of Borders in North America

To put contemporary labor migration from Mexico to the United States in a proper historical perspective, it is necessary to begin at the beginning—well over ten thousand years ago, when people first walked the terrain of the Americas. For the first several millennia of human habitation in the Western Hemisphere, before the establishment of agriculture, territorial boundaries were either fluid or altogether nonexistent. This is because mobility was a necessary component of survival for these human groups, who would have depended on gathering wild plants and hunting animals for food. This is not to say that such groups would not have had boundaries. They likely did, but their boundaries would have been more social or political—"I am a this type of person, they are a that type of person"—than rooted in geographic space.

Beginning about four thousand years ago, fertile land in what is now Mexico began to support large populations with dominant political centers. Eventually the Olmecs, the Maya, the Toltecs, and the Aztecs, among others, built powerful city-states with impressive architecture and well-developed infrastructures. Most of these city-states lacked the defensive structures common in Medieval Europe, but some, like Tenochtitlán, the home base of the Aztec Empire, had defensive structures such as canals and bridges that could be raised—in effect, the Americas' first defended borders. Some of these polities, like the Teotihuacanos, also had cosmopolitan cities with immigrant wards or neighborhoods. To the north, in what is now the United States, there were fewer state-level societies, but powerful chiefly polities abounded; these groups developed expansive trade networks and wealthy market-oriented economies. Many of these polities sought to expand their wealth by incorporating (i.e., conquering) and taxing less powerful groups. Because of this expansionist strategy, pre-Columbian political boundaries throughout North America were less determined by geographical location and more defined by the people who were tribute-paying subjects of the polity.

The arrival of Europeans in the late fifteenth and early sixteenth centuries profoundly transformed the political landscape of the Americas, as different European nations laid claim to the "new" territories. The existing people were largely killed or displaced; survivors were relegated to an inferior status. Spain established "New Spain" and England "New England," and for nearly three centuries the terrain of the Western Hemisphere was ruled over by elites of European descent in the name of European kings and queens. Then, beginning in the late 1700s, battles for independence waged across the Americas. As the colonies fell, national governments rose to take their place and the modern nations of Canada, the United States, Mexico, Guatemala, Peru, Venezuela, and many others were born.

At the time of national independence, the United States was considerably smaller than it is now and Mexico much larger, since Mexico included (what is now) the southwestern United States. The border between the United States and Mexico did not become fixed in its current position until the mid-nineteenth century, when the United States invaded Mexico's northwestern territory as part of its campaign of westward expansion. The subsequent war resulted in U.S. conquest of Mexico's entire northern province (which includes the current states of California, Texas, Nevada, and Utah and parts of Colorado, Arizona, New Mexico, and Wyoming), along with the seventy-five thousand to one hundred thousand Mexicans who lived there.[2] But the establishment of a national border along the Rio Grande in 1854 did not stop people or goods from moving back and forth between the young nations of Mexico and the United States, nor was it meant to.

The Seeds of Globalization: Development and Migration

There is a common misconception that labor migration from Mexico to the United States is fueled by a lack of economic development in Mexico. This understanding of migration is in error, however, because labor migration is generated not by a lack of economic development, but by development itself—and by uneven development in particular.[3] In fact, the movement of labor and goods across the U.S.–Mexico border is and has always been an essential component of the economic development of both nations.

At the time of the Mexican–American War (1846–1848), most Mexicans lived in rural areas and were engaged in locally oriented economic practices. Although there was substantial trade between areas, rural communities tended to be largely self-sufficient in food and other basic necessities. That would change with the presidency of Porfirio Díaz, who took office in 1876. Díaz began implementing liberal development strategies that were geared toward large-scale production and direct foreign investment—particularly from the United States—in Mexico's agriculture, industry, mining, petroleum, and infrastructure.[4,5] Foreign capital investment in agriculture accelerated production, and new large-scale plantations converted cultivation from subsistence goods for local markets to cash crops for export. By the end of Díaz's three-decade reign (1876–1910), five million rural Mexicans had lost their land rights; by 1910, about 70 percent of Mexico's countryside was consolidated in the hands of medium and large landholders.[6]

Liberal development had a powerful impact on Mexico's people. Without land, peasants were no longer self-sufficient in food. Mechanization of agricultural production not only reduced the demand for labor but also depressed wages on the large haciendas—a main source of work for landless Mexicans—while domestic craft producers were undermined by the introduction of mass-produced wares from the United States to local markets.[7] Simultaneously, the costs of living increased, since Mexico was now importing basic foodstuffs. Moreover, as capital investments brought roads, railroads, and agricultural technologies to rural Mexico, the new railroads provided peasants with cheap access to industrializing centers in the cities.[8] As a result, Mexico's cities swelled with rural migrants after 1900. Large reserves of migrant labor put downward pressure on wages in the cities, resulting in violent labor strikes between 1905 and 1910. Eventually, the devastation wrought by Díaz's development policies would help spark the Mexican Revolution, which displaced huge numbers of people and led some two hundred thousand Mexicans to seek refuge in the United States between 1910 and 1917.[9]

Meanwhile, in the United States, growers in the conquered (and formerly Mexican) southern and western territories found themselves experiencing a labor shortage brought on by restrictive immigration policies that cut off labor supplies from China in 1882, then from the rest of Asia in 1917.[10] The Immigration Act of 1917 also curbed immigration of Eastern and Southern Europeans, a main source of labor in the industrial north.[11] To ease the demand for labor, Mexican migrants were exempted from numerical restriction, and an unlimited number of visas could be granted to Mexican workers.[12] To tap this labor reserve, U.S. businesses sent recruiters deep into the heart of Mexico's populated north-central valleys, where they recruited Mexicans to come work in agriculture, construction, and manufacturing in the United States. This system came to be known as *el enganche* (the hook) in Mexico, as peasants were promised great rewards for their labor but were "hooked" into labor conditions that better resembled indentured servitude.[13]

Early Mexican migrants worked in a variety of American industries, including agriculture, mining, railroad construction, and auto and steel manufacturing. By the 1920s, Mexican workers (both migrants and Mexican Americans) constituted as much as 75 percent of the agricultural workforce in California and of the unskilled construction labor force in Texas by the 1920s.[14] As early as 1907, Mexican workers also began migrating to Chicago in large numbers to work in the city's rail yards.In a little over a decade Chicago had amassed the largest population of Mexicans in the United States outside of the U.S. Southwest, and Mexican workers constituted 43 percent of all railroad track labor and 11 percent of employees in steel and meatpacking plants in the Chicago area.[15] The concentration of these industries on Chicago's south side led to the settlement of major Mexican communities in south-side neighborhoods.

As a result of the massive importation of Mexican labor, widespread negative stereotypes about Mexicans, such as their supposed docility, tractability, and uncleanliness, came to be seen as great virtues of the low-wage workforce in the United States. In fact, during U.S. immigration hearings of the early twentieth century, Mexicans were repeatedly identified as a labor force whose racial characteristics made them ideally suited for arduous and low-paying work.[16] Mexican workers were consistently paid less than their white counterparts and were racially segregated from whites in housing, schooling, and public facilities throughout the Southwest.[17] Segregationist legislation was justified by a doctrine of white racial supremacy that cast Mexicans as simple-minded racial "hybrids" of inferior caste to white Americans.[18] Despite increasing American nativism (anti-foreign sentiment) and the establishment of the U.S. Border Patrol in 1924, Mexican migration to the United States reached unprecedented levels in the first decades of the twentieth century and remained high until the onset of the Great Depression.[19]

When the Great Depression froze economic growth in the early 1930s, Mexican migration to the United States came to a virtual halt. In Mexico, the Cárdenas administration (1934–1940) backed away from liberal development policies and instituted substantial social reform, including protection for local producers in the form of import tariffs, foreign exchange controls, labor codes to legalize unions, nationalization of the railroad and oil industries, and social insurance programs. In addition, Cárdenas consolidated rural and urban labor groups under a single political party, the PRI (*Partido Revolucionario Institucional*), ushering in a period of prolonged political stability (and, many would point out, corruption). Perhaps most important, Cárdenas established a policy of import substitution industrialization (ISI), which created markets internal to Mexico and reduced Mexico's dependence on goods imported from the United States.[20]

In the United States, jobs had dried up and Mexican workers were being sent home. U.S. citizens and Mexican nationals alike were rounded up and deported. The number of Mexicans counted by the U.S. census declined nearly 50 percent between 1930 and 1940. At least 415,000 Mexicans were deported, and another 85,000 were "voluntarily" repatriated.[21] The promise of land redistribution combined with social supports and labor reform in Mexico, plus the forcible removal of Mexicans from the United States, slowed Mexican migration to the U.S. nearly to a halt.

The Roots Take Hold: The Breadbasket and the Bracero Program

The decades of the mid-twentieth century are characterized by impressive rates of economic growth in Mexico and the United States.[22] From 1940 to 1970, Mexico's economy grew at an average of 6 percent per year, and industrial and agricultural production grew 120 percent and 100 percent, respectively.[23] This sustained period of growth came to be dubbed the "Mexican miracle," and the health, education, and life expectancy of Mexico's population grew dramatically as Mexico transformed into a relatively wealthy, urban nation.[24]

The *Bajío*, a region that spans Mexico's traditional "sending" states of Guanajuato, Jalisco, Querétaro, and Michoacán, underwent significant modernization, and its agricultural productivity earned it the nickname "the breadbasket of Mexico." Ironically, agricultural modernization actually increased migration, as farmers sought wage work to attain the capital that they needed to make their agricultural output competitive.[25] International migration was thus an important seasonal strategy for farmers seeking supplemental income to bolster their lands' productivity, a task that increasingly required capital input.[26]

In 1942 Mexico signed a binational treaty—the Bracero Program—with the United States that allowed for large numbers of Mexican nationals to work in the United States on a temporary basis. The Bracero Program was considered a win-win proposition for both governments, as it fulfilled the labor needs of powerful agricultural growers in the United States and relieved the pressure of Mexico's large wage-seeking population.[27] Nearly five million Mexican workers crossed the border during the Bracero Program between 1942 and 1964. As millions of Mexican workers became accustomed to employment practices, lifestyles, and consumption patterns in the United States, they established networks between jobs in the U.S. and friends and family members back home that allowed migratory flows to become self-sustaining in the decades that followed.[28]

While the U.S. government was trying to regulate the inflow of Mexican workers under the Bracero Program, employers realized that they could circumvent the costs associated with the program by tapping into the social networks of their Mexican workers. At their employers' behest, braceros could easily recruit brothers, cousins, and friends to come work in the United States outside of the auspices of the Bracero Program as undocumented workers. According to De Genova and Ramos-Zayas (2003:5), as many as four undocumented workers entered for every documented Mexican bracero. In response, the United States launched a high-profile campaign in 1954, called "Operation Wetback," that subjected ethnic Mexicans—citizens and immigrants alike—to heightened anti-Mexican sentiment and deportation. Many Mexican workers became angry, not only at the explicit racial orientation of the sweeps, but at the apparent hypocrisy of the U.S. government, which was condoning the use of Mexican labor "while simultaneously whipping up anti-immigrant hysteria against wetbacks" (Gutierrez 1995:168). In fact, the motive of Operation Wetback was not to reduce Mexican migration but to funnel it through the Bracero Program, creating pressure on the Mexican government to extend the program and giving the appearance to the American public that the border was "under control." In a tag-team effort, the Immigration and Naturalization Service (INS) arrested undocumented workers and transported them across the border to Mexico, where Department of Labor officials were waiting to process the deportees and send them back to work as braceros.[29]

In spite of the economic interdependence between Mexican workers and U.S. businesses that the Bracero Program had established, in 1965 the United States imposed immigration quotas on Mexican nationals *for the first time ever* when the program ended. Initially, a cap of one hundred twenty thousand visas was set for the entire Western Hemisphere, but additional legislation passed in 1976 reduced the number of legal Mexican entries to twenty thousand annually. That is, after encouraging labor migration from Mexico for the better part of a century, U.S. immigration policies slashed the number of visas allotted to Mexicans from an unlimited number to just twenty thousand per year in the eleven years between 1965 and 1976.[30]

Reaping the Harvest: The Political Production of "Illegal Immigration"

As the 1960s drew to a close, Mexico's economic miracle was facing serious challenges. The progress of the past three decades was tainted by growing inequalities between rich and poor, a stagnant agrarian economy, and the blight of urban poverty. By 1970, Mexico owed 4.2 billion dollars to foreign debtors and was, once again, importing basic foodstuffs. Unemployment was rising in both urban and rural sectors, and by 1973 inflation had reached 20 percent; when the government was forced to float the peso in 1976, it promptly lost half its value. The discovery of large oil reserves in 1976 generated revenue and temporarily relieved the pressure of recession, but it simultaneously rendered Mexico more dependent on foreign oil markets. Optimistic about potential future oil revenues, Mexico borrowed huge sums from U.S. banks to buy its way out of the slump.[31]

The price of oil fell in 1982 and Mexico, unable to pay its foreign debts, was forced to default on its loans. In response, the Mexican peso underwent a series of devaluations and ultimately plummeted from 10 pesos to a U.S. dollar in 1981 to 2,300 pesos to a dollar in 1987. Real wages fell by 25 percent between 1981 and 1983; inflation skyrocketed to 480 percent in 1982, and the real value of the minimum wage fell by 20 percent. The prices for essential agricultural inputs like feed, fertilizer, and fuel rose dramatically, and agricultural production in the *Bajío* decreased. Mexico's foreign debt mounted. Adding insult to injury, a 1985 earthquake devastated Mexico City, leaving 20,000 dead and 200,000 homeless. The U.S. government along with financial institutions such as the International Monetary Fund (IMF) and the World Bank stepped in, lending Mexico public funds to bail itself out of the crisis.[32]

Meanwhile, in the United States, a new era in economic policy was dawning. The Reagan administration (1980–1988), along with the World Bank and the IMF, instituted policies that would deregulate and "globalize" economic development. This approach—termed neoliberalism—promoted economic globalization by privatizing public-owned companies, promoting free trade and free markets, and instituting policies that allow, or even favor, the movement of finance and production across national borders. Under pressure, U.S.-educated Mexican leadership responded to the economic crisis by abandoning the centralized state-controlled economy established after the Mexican Revolution and adopting the neoliberal policies of the United States. In 1986 the Mexican government began to sell off government-owned industries to private and foreign investors, scale back regulations on production, relax trade barriers, and generally integrate more fully into the global capitalist system. As the government eradicated price controls and subsidies for local producers, agricultural markets were flooded with cheap, mass-produced American grain. In 1995 Mexico imported nine million tons of grain from the United States, about one third of its domestic consumption.[33]

Mexico's entry into the global marketplace, reinforced and accelerated by the North American Free Trade Agreement (NAFTA) in 1993, was supposed to relieve Mexico's debts and allow the economy to modernize and prosper. Instead, the Mexican economy contracted once again in 1994. Burdened by foreign debt, the government was forced to devalue the peso, prompting global investors to withdraw their money from Mexico's economy (about twenty-five billion dollars total) and slashing the value of the peso in half. Interest rates skyrocketed from 15 to 130 percent. The United States loaned Mexico twenty billion dollars, supplemented by an additional thirty billion supplied by the IMF and the World Bank. Mexico repaid these debts, but its dependence on intra-NAFTA trade—and its susceptibility to global markets—deepened. NAFTA trade networks currently supply over 80 percent of the market for Mexico's international trade.[34]

The economic crises of the 1980s and 1990s had profound implications for Mexican workers and farmers. Among other things, Mexico–U.S. labor migration was converted from a selective strategy employed by a narrow demographic to a widespread strategy to combat a host of problems, including unemployment, low wages, high interest rates, high costs of living, rising crime in the cities, and the inability of local producers to compete with mass-produced American goods. Finally, after years of steady increases, the number of undocumented transmigrants entering the United States from Mexico rose dramatically following the peso crises. For the whole decade of the 1980s an estimated 1.8 million undocumented migrants arrived from Mexico. That number leapt to 4.9 million during the 1990s, and an additional 4.4 million undocumented Mexicans arrived between 2000 and 2005 alone.[35]

In sum, the pursuit of neoliberal economic policy in Mexico and the United States has had three main effects on Mexican workers. First, globalization has put local Mexican producers in direct competition with U.S. industries, driving many Mexican farmers and craftspeople out of business and adding them to the rolls of mobile wage-seekers. Second, it has generated an expanding service economy in the United States that has a seemingly insatiable demand for immigrant labor. Third, the opening of borders to trade and finance, accompanied by the "closing" of borders to workers, has had the effect of illegalizing—but not stopping—transmigrant labor. The combination of these factors largely explains the growth of the undocumented Mexican population in the United States during the last two decades of the twentieth century. Selective enforcement of the border, and the globalization of all aspects of production except for labor, renders the continued migration of labor all but certain. To put it simply, border policies do not stop labor migration; rather, they generate inequality by assigning illegal status to a segment of the global labor force.[36]

Politics of Marginalization

In spite of the pursuit of economic policies that promote globalization and the persistent use of immigrant labor, mainstream political discourse in the United States has taken a decided anti-immigrant orientation over the last three decades. During the 1980s, as the Reagan administration aggressively pursued economic globalization, U.S. policies regarding labor migration—particularly from Latin America—took a decidedly restrictionist turn. Adroitly linking public fears of drug smuggling, Communist invasion, and terrorism to a loosely regulated southern border, Reagan galvanized support for border militarization projects and increased funding for the Border Patrol by 130 percent.[37]

Rising anti-immigrant sentiment culminated in the passage of the Immigration Reform and Control Act, or IRCA, in 1986. IRCA was the first immigration bill directed against illegal immigration, and it expanded the Border Patrol, authorized the president to declare "immigration emergencies," provided long-term undocumented residents in the United States with means to obtain legal permanent resident status, and instituted sanctions on employers who knowingly hired undocumented workers. Although this last provision was the bill's political centerpiece, the wording of the bill released employers from any obligation to check the authenticity of employees' documents and had little impact on the hiring of undocumented workers—though it did create a booming black market in false documents.[38]

The trend toward militarization of the U.S.–Mexico border accelerated during the 1990s. Between 1993 and 1997, the Clinton administration executed a series of border "operations" that "blockaded" sections of the Mexico–U.S. border with fences, floodlights, and other detection technology. Although these operations had no measurable long-term effect in deterring undocumented migration, their symbolic message was powerful. The highly publicized campaigns of Operations Blockade (1993), Gatekeeper (1994), Safeguard (1995, 1999), Hold-the-Line (1997), and Rio Grande (1997) probably did more to create a public perception of the "illegal Mexican immigrant" than anything that had come before. In 1996 Congress passed the harshest anti–illegal immigration legislation to date, the Illegal Immigration Reform and Immigrant Responsibility Act (IIRAIRA). IIRAIRA implemented several restrictionist provisions. First, immigrants who had ever engaged in unauthorized employment became ineligible to adjust their legal status; second, an automatic ten-year bar was applied to anyone in the country for 365 days or more without authorization; third, the standards for visa adjustment became tighter; and fourth, the bill provided new grounds for the deportation of legal permanent residents. IIRAIRA also doubled border enforcement expenditures and restricted noncitizens' (including legal immigrants') access to public resources and further cut the number of legal entries for Mexicans.[39]

The result of these policies is that even undocumented immigrants like Alejandro, Omar, Rene, and Manuel, who have wives and children who are U.S. citizens, largely remain ineligible to legalize their status. To have the automatic ten-year deportation imposed by IIRAIRA waived, undocumented immigrants must leave the United States and return to their country of origin to await a hearing at the U.S. consulate. At their hearing, workers must prove that a ten-year deportation will result in "extreme hardship" for a U.S. citizen; this hardship cannot be emotional, since the pain of family separation is not considered hardship under the law, but must be financial or material. The cases that are most easily approved involve a citizen wife or child who is under medical supervision and relies on the immigrant to provide sole financial support (Dominguez personal communication). Proving a legal case of extreme hardship requires substantial legal work, for which immigrants can expect to pay as much as ten thousand dollars or more, and there is no guarantee that the waiver will be granted. The high cost, high risk, and tight standards of legalization mean that the prospect of becoming a legal permanent resident is currently out of reach for the vast majority of undocumented immigrants in the United States.

Notably, restrictive border policy has not reduced the number of undocumented border crossings, but has shifted migrant routes from more visible, populated areas to more remote and dangerous regions. Since the inception of Operation Gatekeeper in 1994, there has been a 500 percent increase in the number of people who die crossing the border, resulting in more than five thousand migrant deaths.[40] Militarization of the border has had another predictable effect: by making cyclical migration too risky, it has encouraged undocumented people to settle in the United States.[41] This, combined with policies that prevent long-term undocumented residents from adjusting their legal status, has increased the internal, long-term undocumented population of the United States.

The attacks on the World Trade Center and the Pentagon on September 11, 2001, pushed the rhetoric surrounding immigration further to the right by exacerbating nativism and recycling fears about the security of American territory in relation to immigrant workers. Undocumented immigrants became potential terrorists, and loose border policy was hyped as a threat to national security. These fears helped boost proposed anti-immigrant legislation in 2004, 2005, and 2006, as public debates surrounding these proposals sparked a serious wave of anti-immigrant sentiment. Simultaneously, they galvanized an unprecedented mobilization in support of undocumented immigrants. The profile of immigration debates rose throughout the country in early 2006, as did the number of Americans who report immigration as the biggest problem facing the nation—up fivefold, from 2 percent in November of 2005 to 10 percent in May of 2006.[42] Although the American public is nearly evenly split on most major issues of the immigration debate, a significant majority see illegal immigration as a very serious problem.[43] The politicization of immigration appears to have increased the vulnerability of immigrants in particular, and Latinos in general, to discrimination and hate crimes. Surveys of Latinos in 2006 reported that the majority (54 to 76 percent) perceive a rise in discrimination as a result of immigration policy debates.[44] Federal crime statistics indicate that these perceptions are well founded: attacks on Latinos in the United States surged 40 percent from 2003 to 2007.[45]

Politics of Labor Reproduction

Currently, at least twelve million people are estimated to live in the United States without legal authorization, making the undocumented population of the United States the largest in the world. There is no easy way to understand why U.S. immigration policy is so apparently ineffective. At least part of the reason lies in real disagreement among U.S. policy makers about what type of policy is in the best interests of their constituents and supporters. And at least part of the reason lies in the contribution that undocumented workers make to the U.S. economy as low-wage workers.

Undocumented labor is an important component of the U.S. economy and is widely utilized in spite of—or perhaps because of—restrictionist policies. More undocumented males are gainfully employed than any other sector of the U.S. population, and the labor force participation rates of undocumented Mexican men are particularly high—95 percent, compared with 83 percent for U.S.-born men.[46] Although there is broad recognition that undocumented migration is primarily a labor migration, and that most undocumented people come to the United States looking for work, widespread employment of undocumented Mexican workers is tacitly, if not overtly, permitted across the United States.

The relationship between immigration concerns and labor concerns has a long history. At its founding in 1924, the Border Patrol was a small unit of the Bureau of Immigration, which itself was part of the Department of Labor. Indeed, the function of the Border Patrol has never been to stop immigration but rather to regulate flows of Mexican workers by allowing mass importation punctuated by deportations according to seasonal and periodic labor demands.[47] In fact, as the border enforcement arm of Immigration and Customs Enforcement has grown over the past several decades, workplace enforcement has declined. A 2005 *Los Angeles Times* article reported that "from 1993 to 2003, the number of arrests at work sites nationwide went from 7,630 to 445,"[48] and even employers who are caught hiring undocumented people often cannot be prosecuted, because of IRCA's provision that employers must "know" that their employees are illegal. One economist from the University of California, San Diego, told a *New York Times* reporter that "employers feel very strongly about maintaining access to immigrant workers, and exert political pressure to prevent enforcement from being effective." In fact, after a 1998 immigration raid in Georgia, several politicians from the state, including a senator and four members of the House of Representatives, "sharply criticized the [INS] for hurting Georgia farmers."[49]

Undocumented labor—and immigrant labor more generally—continues to be an important component of the U.S. economy. In urban areas of the United States, undocumented workers increasingly labor in an expanding low-end service economy, where they attend to the economically prosperous in industries such as hospitality, maintenance, and construction.[50] The desirability of low-end service workers is often evaluated on subjective criteria such as their "work ethic" and "good attitude," conditions that are promoted by workers' powerlessness. Being particularly powerless, undocumented immigrants make especially desirable service workers, and they comprise over 10 percent of the U.S. workforce in low-end service industries such as groundskeeping and building maintenance (19 percent), construction (17 percent), and food preparation and service (12 percent), though they account for only 5.4 percent of the total civilian labor force.[51] In spite of their elevated participation in the labor force, undocumented workers are more likely to live in poverty than U.S. citizens and are particularly vulnerable to exploitative working relations, poor and/or dangerous working conditions, and economic instability.[52] A prolonged "crackdown" on illegal immigration has also turned into big business for important sectors of the U.S. political economy. In a 2009 article, Tanya Golash-Boza argues that the undocumented status of many immigrant workers benefits at least three groups: politicians who win votes by inciting fear of undocumented immigrants among their constituents, media pundits who boost ratings by railing against "illegal aliens," and contractors who profit from immigration law enforcement expenditures. This "confluence of interests," Golash-Boza argues, helps explain why U.S. politicians doggedly persist in enacting immigration policies that have been proven to fail. While U.S. immigration policies have been ineffective at curtailing undocumented immigration, they have been highly effective at creating a public perception of Mexican and other Latin American immigrants as desperate, dangerous, illegal aliens.

In sum, undocumented migration is neither a historical accident, nor an unintended by-product of authorized migration, nor a result of economic underdevelopment. Rather, undocumented migration is a logical and predictable result of the confluence of three factors: uneven global economic development, the establishment of transnational social networks over time, and policies that restrict legal entries to unrealistic levels.

Notes

1. De Genova 2005; Massey et al. 2002.
2. De Genova and Ramos-Zayas 2003; Gutierrez 1995:13.
3. Portes and Walton 1981.
4. Kirkwood 2000; Massey et al. 2002.
5. This kind of development is known as "liberal" development because it developed in the context of "liberalism," an intellectual and political movement that emerged in Western Europe in the seventeenth century. Liberalism is a "complex of values and practices...that favors progress over tradition, reason over faith, universal over local values, and the free market over government control" (Chasteen 2006:20). Liberalism is also a precursor to "neoliberalism," or economic practices that promote the global spread of free-market capitalism, which is most associated with the United States and England in the late twentieth century.
6. Cardoso 1980; Kirkwood 2000; Massey et al. 2002.
7. Cardoso 1980; Massey 1988; Massey et al. 2002.
8. Cardoso 1980.

9. Kirkwood 2000; Massey et al. 2002:30.
10. Gutierrez 1995; Massey et al. 2002; Ngai 2004.
11. Ngai 2004.
12. Gutierrez 1995; Ngai 2004.
13. De Genova and Ramos-Zayas 2003; Gutierrez 1995; Massey et al. 2002.
14. Gutierrez 1995:45.
15. De Genova 2005; Ready and Brown Gort 2005.
16. Gutierrez 1995; Pedraza and Rumbaut 1996.
17. Gutierrez 1995; Hondagneu-Sotelo 1994; Menchaca and Valencia 1990.
18. Cardoso 1980; Menchaca and Valencia 1990; Pedraza and Rumbaut 1996.
19. Massey et al. 2002.
20. Kirkwood 2000; Weaver 2000.
21. De Genova and Ramos-Zayas 2003:5; Massey et al. 2002:34.
22. Kirkwood 2000; Massey 1988; Massey et al. 1994.
23. Massey et al. 2002:35–36; Weaver 2000:129.
24. Krauze 1997; Weaver 2000:130.
25. Cornelius 1989; Massey et al. 1994; Massey et al. 2002; Roberts 1982.
26. Arias 2004; Cornelius and Martin 1993; Fussell 2004; Preston and Dillon 2004; Roberts 1982.
27. Kirkwood 2000; Massey et al. 2002.
28. Fussell 2004; Massey et al. 2002.
29. Gutierrez 1995; Massey et al. 2002.
30. Calavita 1994; Massey et al. 2002; Mgai 2004:261.
31. Kirkwood 2000.
32. Cerrutti and Massey 2004; Cornelius and Martin 1993; Greider 1997; Kirkwood 2000; Massey 1988.
33. Cerrutti and Massey 2004; Greider 1997; Kirkwood 2000: 206; Portes and Landolt 2000.
34. Centeno et al. 2005; Greider 1997:261–265.
35. Pew Hispanic Center 2006.
36. De Genova 2005; Lipsitz 2005; Massey et al. 1994; Massey et al. 2002; Ngai 2004; Portes and Walton 1981; Sassen-Koob 1981.
37. Massey et al. 2002.
38. Massey et al. 2002.
39. Fragomen Jr. 1997; Maiello and Ridgway 2006; Massey et al. 2002; Porter 2006b; see also Chapter 6.
40. Chacon and Davis 2006: 205, 209.
41. Jimenez 2009; Massey et al. 2002:128–133.
42. Campo-Flores 2006; Swarns 2006.
43. Pew Hispanic Center 2006b; Tumulty 2006.
44. Campo-Flores 2006; Suro and Escobar 2006.

45. Urbina 2009.

46. Passel and Cohn 2009.

47. De Genova and Ramos-Zayas 2003; Massey et al. 1994; Ngai 2004; Sassen 1988.

48. Gorman 2005.

49. Porter 2006a; see also Preston 2006.

50. Characteristics of the service economy and its workforce are not given but are continuously created through state activities and everyday interactions between workers and managers (Gray 2004; Zlolniski 2003). As Gray (2004) points out, there is nothing inherent to the service sector that renders some jobs high-paying and others low-paying. Rather, low wages in the service sector are the function of a confluence of factors, including: lack of unionization, social degradation of low-end service sector jobs, and policies that undermine organization efforts and differentiate sectors of the service labor force by race, gender, and immigration status (Fernandez-Kelly 1983; Fine 1996; Gray 2004; Heyman 2001; Kearney 2004; Stepick and Grenier 1994). Also, Zlolniski (2003, 2006) has shown that the labor flexibility of immigrant workers is not an intrinsic characteristic but is continuously negotiated and challenged in interactions between managers and workers (see also Gomberg-Muñoz 2010).

51. Passel 2006; Passel and Cohn 2009; see also Moss and Tilly 2001; Sassen-Koob 1981; Smith-Nonini 2007; Waldinger and Lichter 2003; Zlolniski 2006.

52. De Genova and Ramos-Zayas 2003; Kocchar 2005; Mehta et al. 2002.

CHAPTER THREE

Jumping and Adjusting To Life Under the Radar

MIGRATION: CHUY'S STORY

I had never really thought seriously about coming to the U.S. I began working with leather when I was twelve years old, and by the time I graduated high school I was making belts and boots—I can do everything but sew them together. I earned pretty good money, like 1,200 pesos [about 100 dollars] a week. My brother and some of my friends were in Chicago and they said they liked it and everything, but I was making good money too, so I didn't need to go to the U.S. like a lot of these other guys.

Then one morning, I think it was a Monday at 7:30 in the morning, my neighbor Mateo came over. He was an older guy and he was actually a U.S. citizen, and he said, "Chuy, come on, we're going to the United States!" And I was like, "What are you talking about?" And he said he was fighting with his wife because she had hid all of his legal papers and he wanted to go work in the U.S. for a while. And so I said, "All right, let's go, let's see what happens." I just decided right there. I thought I would stay for a year then come back home.

I told my mom and she asked me, "You really want to go?" I said, "Yeah, I want to go." And she said okay, then she said a prayer and made the sign of the cross over me, to bless me. That was the last time I saw my mom, nine years ago. After that, we went to the school to say goodbye to Mateo's kids. It was so surreal, so strange.

We took a plane to Tijuana and went to Mateo's uncle's house. The next day, his cousin called some *coyotes* [people smugglers] that he knew, and they came and took us to Mexicali. They brought us to a ranch where a bunch of people were waiting, like twenty-five people, in a house. The coyotes bought us chicken and tortillas, and they sent us to go buy water and bread from the corner store to bring with us. I bought some bread and a gallon of water for me and Mateo.

At first there were men, women, and children, but then the coyotes said, "Okay, all of the women, children, and older people are going first. We're taking you in a van, so you won't have to walk as much." And the men said goodbye to their wives and children, and they left. And there were like fifteen of us left. As soon as it got dark out, another van came, and we all got in. We rode for about twenty minutes before the van dropped us off close to the border. There were no lights, but the moon was bright so we could see.

We got out of the van and the lead coyote said, "You are all going to follow me and do exactly as I say. You have to listen to me because I'm going to tell you how to do it." And we started walking along these dirt and sand paths. We walked in a single-file line, stepping in each other's footsteps, with the lead coyote in front, another coyote in the middle, and the last coyote erasing our footsteps with a branch. The lead coyote was scouting for the Border Patrol and checking the tire tracks of their vehicles. They can tell how long ago their trucks passed and he knew when they would be coming back. We walked like that until daylight, like eight or nine hours.

As we were walking, one of the guys twisted his ankle; he was like fifty years old and he couldn't go on. Mateo told me, "Go ahead, don't worry, I will catch up with you later," and he stayed with the guy. So we kept walking but Mateo and this guy stayed behind.

Mateo had the gallon of water with him, and I had the bread with me in my backpack, so by daylight I wasn't tired, but I was thirsty. As the sun was coming up, we took a break so the coyotes could scout for the Border Patrol. We sat down and I said to the guy next to me, "Do you have any water? I'm really thirsty." He thought about it and said, "You know what, I'm sorry man, but this is all I have." I told him, "It's cool, don't worry about it." Then, a couple of minutes later he told me, "Here man, have some water," and he handed me his bottle of water.

Then the coyotes came back and said that the Border Patrol was coming. They told us to hide and not to follow them if they ran. The lead coyote pointed to some trees in the distance, less than a mile away, and he said, "Wait for it to be quiet, then go to those trees and we will pick you up in a little while. If you get caught, it's okay, we will send someone to Mexicali to get you. Don't worry." Now we could see the trucks getting closer; there were two trucks and a small plane. I hid underneath some bushes, there were four of us hiding under there. Some of the other guys ran but got caught by the Border Patrol. The patrol dogs saw us hiding, but they were leashed and the police were asking the other guys, "How many are you? How many are you?" And they told them, "No, this is all of us, except for two guys that got left behind. One of them is hurt." So they left to go get Mateo and the other guy, and they never saw us.

We ran to the trees and we waited there all day. I took out my bread, and another guy had tuna, and another guy had sweet bread, and another guy had water, so we all shared. And we told our stories, right, of where we were going and everything. One guy had a picture of his son with him, hidden underneath his shirt. I don't think that guy was from Mexico, I think he was from El Salvador, or Honduras, or something, because he didn't want to say where he was from. But we didn't ask, you know?

Early in the morning we had seen a car come by the trees, but we hid because we couldn't tell if it was a patrol car or not. But as it got late, we started to think that it was probably the coyotes, and they had already come and gone. Maybe they didn't know we were there, maybe no one was coming for us. So I told the other guys, "Okay, we have to leave." We started walking toward a highway that was close by, and we thought, "Okay, maybe immigration will find us. Hopefully, immigration will find us, and we can go back to Mexico." But of course, not one patrol car passed by.

Finally, at like eleven o'clock at night, we came across a truck and two guys, two workers from Mexicali who work legally in the fields. And I had the coyote's phone number, so one of the workers called him for us. Twenty minutes later, the coyotes came. They drove us to a house where there were a bunch of people, and the lead coyote told me that Mateo had gone back to Mexico looking for me. He thought I had gotten arrested, and now the coyotes had to cross him again! Ha ha. So Mateo arrived the next day, worried that he would have to pay the coyotes double for crossing him twice, and he is a U.S. citizen!

The coyotes took us all the way to Los Angeles, and from there Mateo and I took a bus to Chicago. When we got to Chicago, one of my friends came to get us and he took us to the apartment where my brother was living with a bunch of other guys. They bought us food and beer, and took us shopping for clothes and shoes. Then, the next day, my brother took me to Il Vino to start working as a busboy.

Life in León

One warm afternoon in León, I asked Chuy's sister to show me which homes on their block had family members in the United States. She shaded her eyes from the sun and began pointing, "This one, this one, this one..."; she turned to face me. "Actually Ruth, I think almost all the people on this block have family in the U.S." For many working-class Mexican men like the Lions, coming of age presents two main choices. The first is to find semi-skilled work in the city, usually in industry, auto repair, or the building trades, or for those who live in more rural areas, to scratch out a living on the family farm. With full-time work and subsidies from the Mexican government, it may be possible to purchase a small home and raise a family. But the Lions say that such a life offers little more than a daily struggle for subsistence, and the second option—going to the U.S. to work—is an appealing alternative.

None of the Lions was the first in his family to move in search of work; their parents or grandparents mostly migrated from the rural landscapes of Guanajuato, Michoacán, or Jalisco to work in León's leather industry. León is a large industrial city with a metropolitan population of just over one million people[1] (roughly equivalent to the size of Dallas, Texas). León's historical downtown area is surrounded on all sides by busy six-lane streets lined with restaurants, shopping malls, and billboards advertising all kinds of leather goods, as well as McDonald's and Walmart. (See Figures 3.1 and 3.2.) Like all big cities, León has richer neighborhoods and poorer neighborhoods, with most areas falling somewhere in between. The poorer neighborhoods in León share a lot of characteristics with the poorer neighborhoods near my home on the south side of Chicago, like graffiti-covered walls and litter-lined streets. But León would never be mistaken for an American city—its brightly painted houses and rutted dirt roads give it a distinctly Mexican appearance. (See Figure 3.3.)

Most of the Lions' fathers work in leather manufacturing, as tanners, shoe makers, shoebox makers, or machinists. For this they are paid an average income of no more than two hundred dollars a week for sixty hours of work. Many of the Lions' mothers and sisters work as well, but typically inside the home, selling cosmetics, stationary, or homemade food; with the little money the women make, they can help buy the family's groceries or school supplies for the children. While this working-class income will meet a family's most basic needs as long as everyone is healthy, it does not easily buy the quality-of-life items that most Americans take for granted, like new clothes, microwaves, cars, computers, or homes with multiple bedrooms. (See Figure 3.4.) More importantly, there is not enough money

FIGURE **3.1 The Plaza Principal in downtown León.** (*Courtesy of the author*)

FIGURE **3.2 Sunrise over the rooftops of historic downtown León.** (*Courtesy of the author*)

FIGURE **3.3 An unpaved residential street in León.** (*Courtesy of the author*)

FIGURE **3.4 A working-class home in León, improved with remittance money.** (*Courtesy of the author*)

left at the end of the week to build any savings, and working-class families in León have very little financial security. To supplement bare subsistence and attain a degree of security, Mexicans in León and throughout the *Bajío* have long relied on remittance money—money sent home from family members working abroad.

Family Strategies

Maria had mixed feelings when her sons, Rene and Chuy, told her that they wanted to go to the U.S. to work. Her own father, Papa Juan, had worked in the United States as a young man, and she remembers helping her mother look after her ten siblings those months that he was away. Now, she worries about their safety and whether she will be able to see them again. Nevertheless, she is proud of her sons, proud that they take such good care of their families and that they have been able to make lives for themselves in the U.S. The money that Rene, and later Chuy, has sent back home has paid for much more than the family's modern appliances. Maria's three daughters have all been able to attain advanced educations, financed by their brothers' remittance money. The oldest daughter is a certified accountant, the middle daughter has just finished her degree in psychology, and the youngest daughter is enrolling in an expensive hospitality program that will qualify her to manage elite hotels in Mexico's tourist zones.

At first glance, many of the Lions seem like lone rangers—young, single men off on a global adventure with only the clothes on their backs and their "willingness" to work hard. Closer inspection reveals that their families are always present—not physically, of course, but in the decisions that they make, and emotionally. The Lions emphasize their strong family ties to their parents, siblings, and wives and children in Mexico. In fact, the decision to migrate in the first place is often made by and for the family. Luis explains that,

> The money situation in Mexico is hard. How can I explain it? You earn money and if you're not married, you have to help out at home. You give money to your parents, or if you have little brothers and sisters, you have to help them. And your nieces and nephews. Everyone who works in the family has to help out, and the little money that you make doesn't go very far.

The remittance money that the Lions send back home is crucial for helping families meet their daily living expenses, purchase homes, finance the education of other children, and support working-poor parents.

Unmarried Lions typically send a substantial portion of their income back to Mexico, about half of which is to be used by the family and the other half of which is saved to be invested in a house or a small business when the worker returns. When workers get married, however, investment tends to shift toward the new nuclear family, and remittances sent to parents diminish.

Alejandro decided to come to the U.S. so that he could help his mom buy a house. He explains that:

> That was the whole plan, you know, that was the whole point. We didn't own a house, we always paid rent and it was a big thing, we always moved from house to house. It's not such a thing as contracts [in Mexico], they'd rent you the house and whenever they decide to kick you out, you had a week or two weeks to find somewhere else. The whole world comes around; the house we have right now we used to live there like in 1985, and my mom loved the house because there was like two houses in one, and we used to live in the top and my aunt used to live in the bottom. They're twins, my mom and my aunt, so they're close and that's why she loved it.

By sheer coincidence, Alejandro met the owner of his old home in Chicago. The house's owner, an undocumented immigrant himself, told Alejandro that he was trying to sell the house, and the two men made a deal. Alejandro's family would be allowed to live in the house while Alejandro made payments on it. It took him ten years to pay the house off, but Alejandro is happy that he could help his mom live securely in the home that she loves.

Alejandro's younger brother, Alberto, has made the trip to the United States three times so far, each time with a goal in mind that, once reached, would hopefully allow him to return to Mexico permanently. But financial security has been elusive for Alberto and his growing family. He explains why he decided to come back to work at Il Vino this most recent time:

> I had a job in Mexico making shoe boxes. With that job you can buy food for your kids, but if you want to go to a park or something, you have to think, I'm going to spend this money and I need it for food, or for electricity. You always live day to day, with just enough for your household bills. But if you need to buy something, like clothes for your family, it's too hard. Or if one of your kids gets sick, or if the water bill, the electric bill, and the rent all come in one week and you need that money for something else, it's too hard. And you always live day to day, under pressure. That's why you say, I'm just going

to go [to the U.S.] for a little while so we can buy something, a little business, small, but just so we have something. But you need money for that. So my wife said to me, 'Maybe you should go for awhile [to the U.S.] again. Work hard and save money, because if you come back in the same situation that you left in, it's not worth it.' That's why I came back here even though I didn't want to.

Luis and Lalo also made the decision to migrate in order to support their wives and children. Luis says that when he first came to the U.S., his goal was to make money to buy nicer things for himself and his family, whom he had left in Mexico. He explains, "In Mexico, all you hear about is how people come back from the United States, and they have a car, nice clothes, they have money and everything. And I said to myself, shit, I want to go to the United States, I want to have a car, I want to have nice clothes, I want to make some money too." But the drug and alcohol addiction that plagued Luis in Mexico worsened here, as he had easy access to drugs and the money to buy them. He neglected his wife and children. Not only did he fail to send money back home, he stopped calling his wife and kept company with other women. Still, he was devastated when he learned that his wife had moved in with another man and wanted a divorce from him. Now, Luis sends money home to his mom, who uses the money to buy food and clothing for her family, and who also keeps tabs on Luis' two boys.

Lalo has managed to maintain a close relationship with his wife and two boys in Mexico in spite of long periodic absences to work in the U.S. The money that he has sent back over the years has mainly been invested in expanding their home in León—which had started out as a one-room building, and now has two floors, three bedrooms, and a modern kitchen. Now, Lalo and his wife would like to open a small restaurant—a *taquería*—in the garage of their home; they hope that the extra income generated by the *taquería*, in combination with Lalo's income as a welder, will allow them to live comfortably—and permanently—together in Mexico.[2]

During long periods in the United States, the Lions spend considerable time and money keeping in touch with their family members back in Mexico. While the telephone continues to be the preferred method of communication—and the phone card business booms in Mexican neighborhoods in Chicago—the more technology-savvy Lions are beginning to take advantage of Internet-based communications. For example, Rene and Chuy recently pooled their money to buy their family in León a computer with a webcam. While the webcam works great, the family's only Internet access is so slow and unreliable that the guys have yet to see their faces live.

Roberto and Leonardo are regulars on networking sites like MySpace and Facebook, where they can swap photos and news with family in Mexico and other parts of the United States. Most often, workers like the Lions "jump" the border to earn more money than they can in Mexico. Oftentimes, their initial goals are concrete and temporary: to buy a house or build a nest-egg to be able to marry. Mexico lacks the credit and mortgage systems that make it possible for working people in the United States to borrow large sums of money to purchase homes and cars, but ten thousand dollars [*dólares*] can buy a nice house in Mexico—mortgage free. With another ten thousand dollars, it may be possible to attain the capital to open a small restaurant, shop, or other family business that can supplement weekly incomes and provide some financial security for a working family.

Since the value of the Mexican peso currently hovers just under one-tenth the value of the U.S. dollar, earning and sending home dollars can multiply a worker's spending power. One returned transmigrant in León explained to me that, "In Mexico, people make a thousand pesos, which is like one hundred dollars, a week. So if you're making five hundred dollars a week in the U.S., you're making five times what you would make in Mexico. And if you can live cheaply, you can send two or three hundred dollars a week home, and it's worth it." Luis says that when he first arrived in the United States he was shocked by his income as a dishwasher at Uncle Luigi's, "I was making three times what I was making in Mexico. I was like 'Wow!' And as a dishwasher! 'Wow!'" Even with only a year or two of work in the U.S., a Mexican worker can substantially increase the chances for long-term financial stability for his or her family.

Because of poor working conditions in Mexico, Mexican workers are often accustomed to long work weeks and arduous, difficult labor. Compared to working in Mexico, many transmigrant workers find that even physically demanding work in the U.S. is less onerous than the work they did back home. One important consideration is the number of work hours—even though Mexico technically has an eight-hour work day, men in León and throughout Mexico routinely work up to twelve hours a day during the week, and another six to eight hours on Saturday. One returned worker in León told me that, "The work [in the U.S.] was easy. Here in Mexico, it's hard. So you get there and you're regularly working eight hours, compared to here, where you work from sunup to sundown." The structure of work in Mexico may make the transition to working in the United States easier for undocumented workers, although, as I discuss in Chapter 5, many new immigrants still have difficulty conforming to the demanding expectations of their labor in the U.S.

Young workers in León also have social incentives to consider migration: while "illegal immigration" is vilified in the U.S., in Mexico, those who "jump" the border earn respect for taking risks to help support their families. Mauricio, a returned migrant, explains: "I think that Mexicans who have worked in the U.S. have more self-respect than Mexicans here, because they want more for themselves. They want more. The guys who stay here, they're scared. Or they're conformists. They're happy with ten dollars a day, and ten dollars the next day. But the ones who go there, they want to progress, they want to make more." As transmigrant workers send money home, they can boost their social stature in communities of origin through remittances and participation in transnational projects.³ Thus, even though undocumented workers face profound stigmatization in the United States, jumping the border may actually increase their status in their home communities.

In addition, while undocumented migration is publicly maligned in American political discourse, there is quite a bit of ambivalence and even tacit approval of it among working people in the United States. One manager at Il Vino says that she used to look down on undocumented immigrants, but since she began working at Il Vino she has changed her mind, "Because I see how they work. I see how awesome they are, how nice they are, how they're just like anybody else." It is not surprising that many American workers who spend their days working alongside undocumented immigrants develop friendly relationships with them. Rene says that he does not feel discriminated against at work because of his illegal status. To the contrary, he says, "They try to help you more, so you can improve yourself. [The bosses] tell us, 'If you need help one day, if you need a lawyer or anything, tell us and we will get you a lawyer.' All companies want Latino workers, they don't care if you're legal or not." While most Lions can point to times in which they have been taken advantage of or otherwise treated badly by Americans, they tend to view those as isolated incidents and do not feel that they experience routine discrimination.

On a broader level, contradictory and confusing U.S. government policy toward unauthorized immigration sends mixed signals to undocumented people. The persistent failure of U.S. policy to enact effective measures to curtail undocumented migration has led immigration scholars to describe U.S. immigration policies as self-contradictory and hypocritical (Massey et al. 2002:104, 105), as it leads many undocumented people to doubt the seriousness of anti-immigrant endeavors. Lalo says that, "Either way, the bosses here need undocumented people. I thought about it—the United States is a very powerful country, if they really wanted to keep people out, they would do it." In fact, undocumented people in the United States can legally do a host of things, including: pay taxes, have bank accounts, purchase homes and cars, and in general be active and productive members of the U.S. economy, in spite of their illegal status. In addition, most local police are prohibited from inquiring about a person's legal status and there is, in general, little risk of being deported for undocumented immigrants who stay "under the radar."

Considering the potential for long-term security, social esteem in Mexico, and the relatively low risk that undocumented work affords, it is not surprising that young men like the Lions routinely jump the border to work in the United States. In spite of the potential rewards, crossing the border without legal authorization is dangerous, and living in the United States without authorization comes at a high price.

The Price of Crossing

Those who "jump" the Mexico-U.S. border face several potential dangers, including: heat stroke, hypothermia, dehydration, armed property owners, immigration authorities, drowning, corrupt Mexican police, street gangs, American and Mexican drug smugglers, robbery, suffocation (usually in vehicles), injury, vigilante violence, sand storms, rape, car accidents, abandonment, and getting lost. Any one of these is potentially fatal.

While building fences sporadically along a 2,000 mile border may be more of a symbolic measure than a serious one, border enforcement projects have had serious implications for undocumented workers. Border militarization has resulted in scores of unnecessary deaths, a predictable outcome of policies that channel migration routes into more remote areas but fail to address the broader processes that compel migration in the first place. According to a September 2009 report issued by the American Civil Liberties Union (ACLU), U.S. border policy has created "an international humanitarian crisis," as more than 5,000 migrants have died along the Mexico-U.S. border since the mid-1990s, on average more than one death per day.[4]

As routes become more dangerous, the cost of crossing also rises, as does immigrants' reliance on each other for aid. In 1993–1994, I worked with a group of young men from Zacatecas who annually paid about two hundred dollars to cross the border with a coyote. The low cost and low risk allowed these men to work for several months or a year in the United States, then return to their homes in Mexico for a few weeks before coming back to the U.S. to resume working. In effect, these men practiced cyclical migration that allowed them to see their parents, wives, and children at least once a year. For most undocumented people, frequent trips across the border are no longer possible. Each time the U.S. makes unauthorized passage more dangerous, the price of crossing rises (see also Massey et al. 2002). In the spring of 2008, Roberto paid a coyote five thousand dollars for his passage back to the U.S.

Such prohibitively high prices mean that any hopeful migrant (who does not have tens of thousands of pesos stashed away) must secure a "sponsor" who is already working in the United States to help pay his passage. All of the Lions were "brought over" by someone else, usually a brother or close friend, who sent them the money to pay a coyote to smuggle them across the border; as Lalo says, "Someone helps you, then you help someone else. It's a chain." In fact, all of the Lions have sponsored the passage of at least one of their friends or family members, and Alejandro and Rene credit themselves with being particularly critical links in the chain that stretches between León and Chicago. This system of sponsorship adds an economic dimension to familial and friendship ties, as undocumented workers continuously incur and repay financial and social debts to each other.

Although most sponsors will help new immigrants secure employment, they have no guarantee that the loan will be repaid. Failure to make good on a loan can have serious social consequences, as bad debtors risk being excluded from the resources of the group. For example, Chuy paid for his friend Perro's passage and got him a job at Il Vino, but Perro was fired and moved to Iowa without repaying Chuy the two-thousand dollars that he owed him. He refused to answer Chuy's phone calls and eventually disconnected his phone altogether. Perro's transgression effectively rendered him "cut off" from the resources of this social network. Perro can no longer expect to receive any aid from Chuy or the other Lions; he is an outcast. In fact, the social repercussions of failing to repay a debt can extend all the way back to Mexico. After Perro changed his telephone number, Chuy began calling Perro's mother in Mexico. Chuy explains that Perro's mother will be embarrassed by her son's irresponsibility and will put pressure on him to pay Chuy his money. After this "bad loan," Chuy doubts that he will take the chance of sponsoring anyone else. Rene, who sponsored Chuy and three other friends, says that as the cost goes up, it is harder and harder for him to find the extra money to loan to his friends.

Life Under the Radar: Papers

With thousands of dollars on the line, it is in the interest of the sponsor to help the new immigrant secure employment as soon as possible. Much like an indentured servant, newly arrived undocumented immigrants often spend their first few months in the United States working just to pay for their crossing. New undocumented immigrants typically get jobs through a working friend and then go "get papers" so that the employers can produce the requisite paperwork if needed. It is relatively rare for an undocumented immigrant to work completely "under the table" without documents of any kind; the majority use a social security number and pay taxes, but the social security number is typically either random or was issued to someone else.[5]

"Papers" is a catch-all term that refers to the documents that unauthorized immigrants use to secure employment and get by in the U.S. Papers usually include a social security card (either real or counterfeit, usually around $50) and, if the undocumented immigrant has lots of money to spend, may also include a legitimate Drivers' License or State ID, credit cards, health insurance cards, and anything else one typically finds in a wallet (this more expensive package can cost hundreds of dollars). Papers are not hard to get. I once went with an undocumented worker to obtain papers that he needed for a new job. We pulled into a parking lot, having made no previous contacts with anyone, and two hours and one hundred and forty dollars later, he had obtained a brand new counterfeit social security card and counterfeit driver's license with his name and picture on them.

When it comes to getting papers, undocumented immigrants have two main choices, each with its own risks and benefits. Some workers choose to purchase legitimate documents that have belonged to someone else. That is, they assume the identity of a citizen or legal resident and use his or her information to secure employment. The benefit of this strategy is that the employee's name and social security number match government records; this helps protect the immigrant from "no-match" letters. No-match letters are notices sent by the Social Security Administration (SSA) to employers that inform them when employees' social security numbers cannot be matched to SSA records. Although the SSA notes that it cannot share this information with other Federal agencies and has no enforcement authority,[6] these letters have been wielded by employers to subdue and fire undocumented workers in recent years. Thus, it is in undocumented workers' interest to avoid no-match letters, though there are also serious drawbacks to using someone else's name and social security number. If the immigrant becomes eligible to "fix" his status, there is no paperwork in his own name, no record of his employment or tax payment. More importantly, assuming someone else's name and using their social security number renders the immigrant vulnerable to charges of identity theft, a felony crime. Lastly, real documents are significantly more expensive than counterfeit ones and have very limited utility.

The other, more popular option is for an undocumented immigrant to get papers that display his own name with a made-up social security number—counterfeit papers. The major drawback of counterfeit papers is that the worker is vulnerable to no-match letters. Also, police can detect real government IDs from counterfeit ones, so the counterfeit IDs are no good for driving, or anything else for that matter, beyond securing a job. However, this strategy does allow a worker to get a job under his own name and leave a paper trail of employment and tax payment, which may be helpful if he intends to change his legal status.

One of the Lions has acquired a TIN (Taxpayer Identification Number) under his own name. This is a legitimate government-issued number that allows a worker without a social security number to pay taxes. This worker has had to ask Il Vino to "re-hire" him under his TIN number after he had initially secured employment with a fraudulent social security number, though the TIN does not confer employment eligibility. Since getting a TIN number is the closest thing to legitimate documents that an undocumented worker can get, an increasing number of them are choosing this strategy. Even though most undocumented immigrants have to get "papers" to get a job, they rarely use their fraudulent papers in any other circumstances. Instead, most undocumented Mexican immigrants have a "*matricula consular*," a consulate ID issued by the Mexican government that identifies the holder as a Mexican national. With a *matricula* ID, immigrants can open a bank account, buy a car, verify their age, and register for adult education classes. (See Figure 3.5.) The *matricula* does not, of course, give them authorization to drive in the U.S. or to work.

Life Under the Radar: Getting Adjusted

Crossing the border is just the first challenge for undocumented workers in the U.S. At least initially, their physical movements are often severely limited by language barriers, unfamiliarity with their surroundings, and fear of capture by authorities. Omar explains that life in the U.S. is more difficult than life in Mexico because, "You come here with nothing. And it's scary to start working, because it's so different here. For example, in Mexico you know what to do, you know how to look for a job, but here, you don't know how to do anything." Self-consciousness about being different can intensify a new arrival's sense of isolation, as can English-language difficulties. Alejandro says that when he first came to Chicago,

FIGURE **3.5 A Chicago-area bank advertises that it accepts the** *matrícula* **ID as identification.** (*Courtesy of the author*)

> I was so hungry one day, and this guy [that I was living with] knew English and I asked him, "You know what, I'm starving, can you come with me to get something to eat?" And he was like, "What, you don't know English? That's your problem." So I said to myself that day, I will learn English and when somebody needs me to go translate I will do it. Every time somebody comes to me like, "I got pulled over and they took my car"—there's times people call me at four in the morning because they got pulled over. And I was there. I was never like, "Screw you." Because that happened to me and I didn't like it.

For Lions who plan to stay in the United States only briefly and then return to their homes in Mexico—like Alberto and Lalo—there is little incentive to learn English and make Chicago their home. They tend to limit their movements to neighborhoods with high concentrations of Mexican immigrants, and they remain largely segregated from wider society. For Lions who have lived in Chicago for many years, are proficient in English, and have families in the United States—like Alejandro, Manuel, and Rene— there is a higher degree of comfort moving about the city and participating in Chicago's social life. Rene, for example, likes to take his family to Cubs games and to Navy Pier in the summer, while Alejandro and his girl-friend enjoy downtown Chicago's restaurant scene. Rene, Roberto, Chuy, Leonardo, and Alejandro have all studied English as a Second-Language (ESL) at a nearby community college to ease their time in the United States.

But even for Lions who have little difficulty integrating socially in wider society, their primary social group consists of friends from León.

While migration to the United States disrupts traditional household arrangements and threatens undocumented immigrants with emotional isolation, cultivating friendships with other workers helps guard against that isolation. Even though they work together fifty or more hours each week, the Lions also spend much of their time away from work socializing with one another. Rene, Roberto, and Chuy usually make dinner together on Sundays, while housemates Alejandro, Alberto, Luis, and Carlos like to stay up late, talking and drinking beer. Though the Lions miss their families most intensely on holidays such as Christmas, they spend these rare days off together, preparing traditional Mexican dinners, playing card games, and listening to music. (See Figure 3.6.) Luis says that when he began working at Uncle Luigi's, friendship bonds helped him get through the first few months of work: "Everyone was Mexican, and when I get there it was, 'What's up, brother?' 'How you doing?' 'Where are you from?' And you talk with people, you know, 'I'm from here,' you know, so we made friends. And that's how you get by at work." For the Lions, cultivating a transnational social network that turns friends from

FIGURE **3.6 Roberto, Manuel, and Rene celebrate the 4th of July, and a rare day off, with a picnic at the beach.** (*Courtesy of the author*)

home into coworkers and housemates helps supply crucial material and emotional resources. Luis notes that, after the initial elation with making dollars passes, getting adjusted to life in the U.S. involves accepting the drudgeries of workaday life. He says,

> Eventually you realize that it's the same shit. You're working just to get by and it's the same as [in Mexico]. Sure, I'm making dollars, but I'm spending dollars too. You have to pay your bills, your rent, you have to buy your food, you have to wash your clothes. You know, everything you have to do in Mexico you have to do here. It's the same, the only difference is that here it's the U.S. and there it's Mexico.

Perhaps the most critical difference between living in Mexico and living in the U.S. is having to manage the risks associated with illegal status. Being undocumented impacts everyday, routine activities—particularly getting around. The Lions are not eligible to get valid drivers' licenses, although as suburban residents they invariably have to drive to get to and from work. The risk of not having drivers' licenses is compounded by consequent ineligibility for insurance coverage (though their vehicles are typically covered), which makes driving even more stressful. Being stopped by police will mean a hefty fine, a court date, and an impounded vehicle for unlicensed drivers. Getting a vehicle out of the impound requires getting the car released to its owner, who must produce a driver's license. For this reason, the titles to Lions' vehicles are held by U.S. citizens whenever possible. For Lions who aspire to home ownership, being undocumented means either taking out a mortgage with a high interest rate—because people without valid Social Security numbers do not qualify for the best loans—or having the loan held in the name of a citizen spouse or relative. This makes undocumented people especially dependent on and potentially vulnerable to their citizen family members, a vulnerability that can disrupt family relationships. One undocumented parent said that he is afraid to discipline his teenage daughter, who has threatened to call immigration authorities on him if he does not allow her to stay out at night with her friends.

Fear of detection by authorities affects broader behaviors, as undocumented people are careful to "fly under the radar" at work and in society at large. This is one reason why undocumented workers tend to have such "good attitudes"—being confrontational with the boss may put them at heightened risk for detection, as bosses have been known to call immigration authorities on their own employees. Former migrant worker Ivan explains that, "What happens is that Mexicans or Central Americans who go illegally are scared, scared of the *migra* [immigration authorities], of the police. So, they keep a low profile so they won't have problems with anybody. The difference between Mexicans and other workers is that Mexicans always keep a low profile and keep their mouths shut." Lalo agrees and says that, as an undocumented worker, "You know that you have to do [what is asked of you], you come here to work, [and] you have to do what they tell you to do." Relatedly, undocumented people have little protection from unscrupulous employers who take advantage of them by not paying them, not providing required safety protections, or refusing to take care of undocumented employees who are injured on the job. This last situation happened to Luis, who fell on an unsafe construction site and injured his back. His employer not only refused to cover Luis' medical expenses, but fired him, explaining that Luis' injury made him a liability. Angry but resigned, Luis paid for a few sessions of physical therapy on his own then began looking for another job.

Changing Ideas of Home: Return Migration and Return-Return Migration

While most transmigrant workers from Mexico come to the United States with a temporary goal in mind and plan to go back to Mexico once it is reached, over time goals change, new expenses arise, and the conception of "home" itself can shift. This is especially true when so many people from the same area migrate that entire communities become substantially relocated from Mexico to the U.S. For example, the last time that Rene went back to León to visit, he was bored; he had expected to see all of his old friends, but there is no one left in his neighborhood. He says,

> It's not the same in Mexico now. I mean, life is better in Mexico, but after you've been here for a while, being there again is hard to get used to. Before I came here the first time I had a lot of friends in León, you know, and I would hang out in a lot of different places. But after I was here for three and a half years, I went back to Mexico and I would go to those same places, but there was no one there. Everyone was here.

When I met with Roberto in León in the spring of 2008, he was also restless. Going from an active work and social life to one in which he has nothing to do during the day was nice at first, he said, but was beginning to get on his nerves. He explained, "When I come to the United States it's like going to the factory and when I go to Mexico it's like going home again for the weekend." Though he had a nice visit with his family, Roberto soon returned to Chicago and to his job at Il Vino.

Like the rest of the Lions, Leonardo grew up in a modest house in a working poor neighborhood of León. He is the youngest of nine children, all of whom were supported on his father's weekly salary of about 150 dollars, which he earned as a machine worker in one of León's many shoe factories. Leonardo says that his family lived "regular," not poor but not rich either, and as a teenager Leonardo began working to help pay his own way. He learned to paint cars, a job that paid about 100 dollars a week for fulltime work. At nineteen, he decided to move to the United States to "get ahead" [*superarse*], since his income was too modest to enable him to buy a house in Mexico. Leonardo says that he did not want to be like his brothers, who got married but had to bring their wives to live at his parents' house because they could not afford a home of their own. For more than five years, Leonardo has been sending a portion of his earnings back home to Mexico, part of which goes to help support his parents and part of which goes into a savings account to pay for his future home. Finally, Leonardo is ready to begin construction on the house, but now his goals have changed. He has met a girlfriend in Chicago, a nursing student and waitress, and the two have gotten serious. Now, Leonardo is unsure whether he will return to Mexico or make his life here; for now, the construction is on hold.

Some transmigrants who achieve their temporary goals return to Mexico and settle there permanently. For Ivan, who lived in the U.S. for ten years and established a successful landscaping business, Mexico offers a better quality of life than the debt-oriented culture of the United States. He says that,

> There [in the U.S.], it's easy to make money, they give you credit, and you can get a car, then you get a house. And after a few years, you get a better car, or a better house, but now you're working to pay for that. And it's like a chain, and you get used to it. So you're always in debt, but they make it easy for you to keep paying…it's a kind of slavery. You think you need that stuff, and you will keep working to keep paying for it.

Ivan says that he prefers living in Mexico, debt-free, and he has used the money that he saved to build a nice home on the outskirts of León. He is working as a truck driver and, even though he makes far less money than he did in the U.S., Ivan says that he is going to try to make it in Mexico. He believes that his familiarity with English, his work experiences in the U.S., and the esteem that he gets from being a transmigrant, will help him build a successful landscaping business in León.

Other return migrants are more ambivalent about their lives in Mexico. During my time in León, I paid a visit to Mauricio, a long-time Il Vino busboy and an old friend of the Lions. As I located his house on a street map of León and plotted my course to his neighborhood (creatively named "León 1"), my hostess grew so concerned that she insisted her daughter accompany me to the interview. While I thought such precautions were probably unnecessary, as I drove through León 1's garbage-strewn and potholed dirt streets, past open sewers and crumbled houses, I was glad for the company. I found Mauricio living in a very small one-room building that he shares with his wife and their infant son, his brother, his aunt and uncle, and two young cousins. There were sheets hung up to create "rooms," but the house was undeniably cramped.

Mauricio was a two-time transmigrant worker in the United States. The first time that he went to the U.S., he was recruited by Alejandro, Alberto, and Rene to work as a busboy at Uncle Luigi's. He stayed for five years before returning to Mexico. He spent a full year in Mexico, without working at all, and then returned to Chicago, his friends, and his busboy job. After two years, Mauricio went back to Mexico to marry his long-time girlfriend, and he has stayed in Mexico ever since. In spite of his modest surroundings, Mauricio says that he has been able to work steadily as a salesman, and that overall he is happier in Mexico. He says, "I'm making pretty good money, like $180 a week, and my house and my car are paid off, so, yeah, it's fine what I'm making. Here, the work is slower, life is more tranquil." Mauricio hopes to return to Chicago someday and bring his wife, but he has no immediate plans.

I again provoked my hostesses' consternation when I planned a trip to the neighborhood of Chapalitas to interview Alberto and Alejandro's brother, Rigo (Chapalitas apparently has a reputation for kidnapping gangs). From the patio of Rigo's two-story home—the very same house that Alejandro bought for his mother and her sister which is shared by Rigo, his wife and two children, his mom, his aunt and her family, and Alberto's wife and three daughters—Rigo talked about the difficulty of "making it" in Mexico. After eight years as a busboy, first at Uncle Luigi's and then at Il Vino, Rigo returned to Mexico and has been working in an assembly plant that manufactures shoeboxes. He works ten to eleven hours each day, Monday through Saturday, and brings home the equivalent of one hundred and twenty dollars weekly. He says, "That's a lot of hours for little money. With what I make now we have just enough for food and our daily needs. We had a car, but we had to sell it because we didn't have enough money." In contrast, when he was working as an Il Vino busboy, Rigo was sending home about two hundred and fifty dollars a week, or more than double what he currently earns. As Rigo finds it difficult to make ends meet for his family, he said that he will probably go back to Chicago, "I want to, I don't know when, but yes, I want to go back." As I get ready to send this book to press, I have recently heard that Rigo has just arrived in Chicago and is already back to work at Uncle Luigi's.

One fact highlights the degree to which these workers' lives have become truly and probably permanently transnational: the workers in Mexico mostly say they want to come back to the United States, and the workers in the United States mostly want to return to Mexico. Close relationships with friends and families in both Mexico and the United States mean that the Lions will forever emotionally reside in both places.

Notes

1. http://www.e-local.gob.mx/work/templates/enciclo/guanajuato/ municipios/11020a.htm
2. But see the Epilogue.
3. See Cohen 2001, 2004; Smith 2006; Stephen 2007.
4. Chacon and Davis 2006; Jimenez 2009; Massey et al. 2002.
5. Massey et al. 2002; Porter 2006b.
6. http://www.ssa.gov/legislation/nomatch2.htm

CHAPTER FOUR

Múy Unidos
Friends, Networks, and Households

HAVING FRIENDS MAKES THINGS EASIER: ALEJANDRO

My name is Alex, and I'm thirty five years old. I came from León, Guanajuato, Mexico when I was sixteen, so in 1989, almost twenty years ago. I started working when I was seven years old. That was my dad's idea, to learn to be responsible. There was not too much I could do when I was seven, but just like bring the tools to the guys and stuff. Later I worked in a tire shop, doing alignments, balance. I became a professional at balancing, I went to school for it. But the pay was like nothing you know, if you're talking about dollars, it'd be thirty dollars a week.

So when I came to Chicago I went from making thirty dollars to a hundred and fifty dollars a week and I was like, "Yeah!" I started working as a dishwasher and then within a month they put me on as a busboy. And as a busboy you had a day off, and it was like ten dollars more per week. And you were like, "Oh my god," you know, "I have a day off!" But there's not too much you could do if you don't know the language and you don't have a car.

My mom's brothers were here, but as soon as I got here I didn't see them much, I was by myself. And my dad was here, so I was saying to myself, "Oh my dad is here, my uncle is here, so I'm set." But the day I got here my dad told me, "Oh you're gonna work here, you're gonna live here, I'm leaving." So he left. He hooked me up with a job but not with secure pay. Just to get me a job he told the managers, "Just try him out, if he works you can pay him, if not then he'll learn." They didn't pay me for the first month. I was working twelve hours a day, not a day off.

At that time the restaurant gave you a place to live. That was the only way that I survived. That's the way they used to do it before, most of the restaurants provided a place to live, six or seven Mexican guys to an apartment. I went to a couple other restaurants and it was pretty much the same, the pay was low, like really, really low. At that time I was working like seven days a week, twelve hours a day for like a hundred and fifty dollars a week. It was low. But when you come from Mexico, even this low you still think it's a lot, because you compare the money there.

We're all friends and it's like a chain. I think I was the creator, I came here first and everybody followed me. But everybody started coming in after Johnny's [a local restaurant]. At Johnny's they decided not to give us a house anymore and the pay was not enough to pay rent, so that's when I moved to Uncle Luigi's. So we all moved to Uncle Luigi's and then we worked there for a year or two and more people started coming from our town. From me being by myself it got to a point where there were like twenty of us. And it's always been the same thing, like we were working at Uncle Luigi's and then everybody moved to Il Vino, everybody came to Il Vino.

Having friends makes things easier. It doesn't cover the hole that you have, if you're missing your family, if you have a girlfriend or a wife, it doesn't cover it but it helps. It helps get your mind off of it. Like if you have a day off and a couple of other people have the same day off, you go and do something together, it takes your mind off. Because I used to have a day off when I first came here but I had no friends. It was hard because I would come home and be by myself in a room, just thinking, and it was difficult. You're constantly thinking, why am I doing this? But what kept me going was what I wanted. So that's what I compare, that time by myself to now that other people are here, and it makes a difference. Just by hanging out, you know, even coming home. We used to come home at eleven or midnight and we would go to sleep at four o'clock in the morning. We would make dinner and watch movies or play video games and nobody would go to sleep.

In spite of physical separation from place of origin and, often, family and friends, many immigrants are deeply embedded in transnational social networks that provide them with crucial material and emotional support.[1] Immigrant workers with resources can make frequent visits to their home countries, where they reconnect with old friends and family. For undocumented immigrants in the U.S., the dream of returning home is increasingly just that—a dream. As the U.S. further militarizes its southern border and intensifies criminalization of undocumented immigrants, fewer workers can move physically between the U.S. and Mexico with any frequency. Instead, these workers spend years and even decades in the United States without physical contact with their families and home communities. To compensate for this loss, they seek belonging here in the U.S., comforting themselves with the company of friends, girlfriends, and frequent communications home. The Lions also utilize these social contacts to evaluate jobs and bosses and maximize their working and living conditions. This chapter explores how the Lions are embedded in social networks and households and how they access the emotional and material resources these bonds provide.

Utilizing a Social Network: Finding Work

The social circumscription of undocumented workers results in an increased reliance on fellow undocumented immigrants for aid and assistance. Even workers with family members who are legal U.S. residents or U.S. citizens often find themselves dependent on their undocumented networks, as legal-resident family members may be wary of helping an illegal relative if they believe it could have negative repercussions for them. Lalo explains how intensified anti-immigrant policies have narrowed his social resources, making people like him more and more reliant on immigrant networks:

> If you have a relative who has papers and you tell him, "You know what? I'm here at the border, I'm in the U.S., I just don't have a place to go and I want you to help me," they might tell you, "You know what, I can't let you come here." So you look for help from the other side, from someone who is not your relative, and those people help you more than your own family.

Undocumented immigrants will often use their social networks to get a lead on an available job before they even leave Mexico. Since workers are often the first to know that a coworker is leaving and a job will become available, they may have a friend or family member in Mexico lined up as a replacement before the boss even knows a change is coming. All of the Lions have gotten jobs by tapping into the resources of their social network, and they have all recruited coworkers through their network.[2] Luis explains, "You come here and don't know anybody, you don't know anyone except the guy who brought you, or maybe some people from your town. So what gets you around are the other guys, the other wetbacks who get you a job, 'Hey, I got this job, come here to work.' Cool. And then another guy comes, 'Hey, this job pays better, come over here.'" At Il Vino, the Mexican workers have almost exclusive access to information about which busboys are leaving or will not work out. As Rene explains, they diffuse this advance knowledge throughout their social network, and when it comes time for the worker to leave, the other busboys have a suitable replacement all lined up: "We would tell [the boss], 'He's going to Mexico, can we bring this guy in [to replace him]?' and he would say, 'Yeah, bring him.' And then the next year another guy would leave for Mexico and we would bring in somebody else." Occasionally, employers will encourage their workers to take an even more direct role in the recruiting and hiring process. Alejandro explains that at Uncle Luigi's,

> [The managers] said we're opening a new place over there and you been with us for a long time, so come and work with us and you be in charge of the busboys. So I went over there but there was no busboys, I was the only one. So I started making phone calls and asking my friends from León, "Do you want to come work over here?" ...So I called them and everybody started going over there. We started with two and then they would bring another two you know, like cousins and friends, but everybody from León.

This arrangement has advantages for both the workers and the boss. For undocumented workers, who often count on each other to share living expenses, transportation, and who may have invested in the new immigrants' passage, securing income for a new arrival makes good financial sense. It also helps the group, which is bound by legal status, language, and common origin, monopolize job opportunities and maintain their autonomy. A friend or family member is also more likely to feel invested in the existing group than a stranger and so, from the outset, is considered trustworthy and more likely to conform to group norms. The increased comfort that the Lions feel working with people that they've known for a long time and trust should not be discounted as an additional incentive for bringing in people from "back home."

For the boss, letting your workers take charge of the hiring process cuts down on the investment required to find a suitable new employee. If a boss is pleased with his staff it makes sense to hire more workers who share the same background and social network, and likely the same values and attitudes toward work. Also, when the existing workers feel invested in a new worker, and when they have the same native language, the boss can feel confident that the new worker will be properly trained in both the mechanics of the job and the work culture of the existing employees. As this quote from an Il Vino manager indicates, management is quite aware that it is in the workers' interest to properly train and socialize new busboys to be hard workers; she says, "With us, [the Mexican immigrants] bring their friends, they bring their family. And I don't think that they're going to bring their friends and their family if they're not going to be fantastic workers, because they know that's who they're going to be pooling [tips] with at the end of the night. They know they're a reflection of them." Of course, the boss is the ultimate authority who can—and does—give and withdraw permission for the workers to hire and train amongst themselves.

Many U.S. employers have become quite adept at tapping into undocumented social networks to recruit new workers. Leonardo explains that not long after his arrival in Chicago, he went to visit a friend at Uncle Luigi's, "And the boss, he's American, and he said, 'Hey, amigo, did you find a job yet?' I told him no. 'Do you want to work?' 'Yes.' He said, 'Tomorrow come to our other location, you can work there.' And so I went the next day and he gave me a job." Tony and Colleen were part-owners of several restaurants before they opened Il Vino, giving them access to lots of potential experienced restaurant employees. When Il Vino opened, Tony and Colleen tapped into these employment networks to recruit the "best staff" that they could find. Rene heard about Il Vino directly from Tony, who was a regular at the restaurant where Rene worked. Tony recruited Rene to come and help with the construction of Il Vino; he did, and when Il Vino opened, Tony offered Rene a cleaning job. Rene accepted and worked briefly as a janitor before being promoted to busboy. He has been working as a busboy at Il Vino for eleven years and, for most of that time, his fellow busboys have mostly been friends and acquaintances from his hometown of León.

Money and Respect: Assessing Jobs and Bosses

Social networks not only provide information about immediate opportunities, but also supply a collective pool of information and experience which network members draw on to make decisions about work and living situations. Like a potluck dinner, every member brings his own connections and resources to the network, which other members of the group can then access; immigrant households and workgroups are thus vital social nuclei for passing information and opportunity through a larger social network. The Lions use this collective information to take advantage of existing opportunities and to improve their situations.

The Lions are quite savvy about constraints on their job opportunities, and they assess jobs as desirable or not relative to their other options. That is, an available job as a busboy or a line cook isn't compared to, say, an engineering job or a nuclear physicist position—these are simply not within the realm of possibility. Rather, a job opportunity in a restaurant might be evaluated in comparison to landscaping or janitorial jobs, which tend to be more accessible to undocumented immigrants. The Lions harbor few illusions about the type of employment they are likely to get. When Lalo's sixteen-year-old son, Armando, told Lalo he wanted to come to the U.S. to work with him, Lalo advised him to stay in school in Mexico because, "Here [in the U.S.] the only jobs you're going to find are dishwasher, busboy, kitchen, in construction, in landscaping." Armando decided to migrate anyway and, just as his dad predicted, he currently works in a restaurant kitchen as a dishwasher.

Undocumented Mexican workers are aware not only of what kinds of jobs are accessible, they know which companies hire undocumented workers. There are cues that employers give to indicate their willingness to hire undocumented immigrants, and a company can quickly become known as a place that either does or does not hire undocumented workers. The most secure way of knowing that a place is "safe" for undocumented workers is to know undocumented people that are employed there. At restaurants like Il Vino and Uncle Luigi's, when an existing busboy brings in a friend to work, the owners may not ask the friend for his social security card right away. Instead, they often tell the existing busboy that the friend is hired, but he needs to go get his "papers" and come back the next day. In this way, the owners acknowledge the undocumented status of the new employee and give their tacit approval of it.

The second most important concern when evaluating the desirability of a job is pay. Pay considerations include dollar amount per hour or week, whether pay is hourly or salaried, how many hours a week are available to work (if pay is hourly, the more the better), and whether workers are paid by check or cash. If the ultimate goal of the worker is to "fix" his legal status he might prefer to be paid by check; conversely, if the worker's goal is to make as much money as possible and then return to Mexico, he will probably prefer a cash job. Cash-only jobs are fairly rare: Massey et al. (2002:124) report that, in 1998, 20 percent of undocumented immigrants reported cash income; a more recent report from the Social Security Administration estimates that about 25 percent of undocumented immigrants work for cash only (Porter 2005). In the restaurant industry, most service employees (citizens and immigrants alike) are paid with a combination of payroll checks and cash tips.

In restaurants, Mexican immigrant workers often start out in the lowest paid position of dishwasher, then work their way up to line cook, salad preparation, or busboy.[3] The possibility of "moving up," or being rewarded for work with better opportunities, is an important consideration when evaluating a job. Before he started at Il Vino, Lalo worked at a Chinese restaurant and says that he appreciated the owners' willingness to reward his hard work: "I started there as a dishwasher, then they put me on food prep cutting vegetables, so I had moved up and they paid me a little bit more." Another important consideration when evaluating a job is respect. Busy restaurants are high-stress environments, and it is not uncommon for managers to be verbally abusive to employees (see also Fine 1996). Undocumented workers make particularly easy targets; as Alejandro makes clear, this is a vulnerability that they are aware of and strive to avoid:

It's just the whole point that you have no papers and they can fire you at any minute. If it's a white guy and they fire him for no reason, he can sue them. You can use race and discrimination, but if you have no papers you're afraid to do anything legal against anybody because you might be the one paying for it. The owners know that, so they can yell at you, scream at you, even call you names and you take it. There's nothing you can do.

Since undocumented workers are especially vulnerable to exploitation and abusive treatment, the Lions value a job in which their work is appreciated and they are treated well by management and coworkers. Luis explains, "What makes a good boss is knowing how to treat people, like giving them opportunities to move up, or treating you well, not yelling all the time and on top of you. It's what I told you, if he sees that you work well, he changes toward you. It's a way to thank you for your work, he gives you opportunities. That's what makes a good boss, more than anything." Lalo agrees and says that one of the things he liked best about his former job as a cook was that, "Every year they would give us a bonus. It wasn't a lot, but it showed that they cared about us, at work, you know. And so you would work harder." The quality of a job, and the dignity of immigrant workers, largely depends on whether those in charge cultivate an atmosphere of friendliness and respect toward the immigrant staff. This can vary greatly from place to place. The Lions agree that the staff and customers at Il Vino largely treat them with respect. In fact, Alberto says that the thing he likes most about working at Il Vino is the friendliness of the staff. He explains, "Everyone, all of the waiters are good people, they say hi to you, they never give you dirty looks or yell at you, they treat you well. Everyone there is good people and so you feel good working there, you feel comfortable."

Autonomy is another important characteristic of a good job. The Lions explain that autonomy and trust go hand in hand and often must be earned over time. Alberto says that when his brother-in-law Luis first started at Il Vino, he aroused Tony's suspicion by entering and leaving the liquor storage room for no apparent reason:

> And the owner came and said to me, "Hey, what's going on?" I said, "Why?" He said, "Why is this guy hanging around back here?" I said, "No, it's nothing, he's looking for the keys to the gate." And he searched the room to make sure there wasn't a bottle lying around that he was going to steal. He said, "He didn't steal anything?" I said, "No, I'm right here, how is he going to steal? He didn't steal anything." He said okay and he left. It's like he never trusts new people but if he sees me going in and out of the liquor room he never says anything. Like he trusts that I'm not going to do anything wrong, you know? That they trust me, I think, is the first thing that makes you feel good. When they're always checking what you're doing, you don't like it. Always behind you, over your shoulder. But no, here they let you do what you know how to do.

Tony's confidence that Alberto is trustworthy means that Alberto has some degree of autonomy on the job; he does not have to worry about being constantly watched. Autonomy, and the greater freedom, trust, and responsibility it entails, is vital to workers' sense of dignity and is an important characteristic of a desirable job.

The social atmosphere and relatively high pay at Il Vino also make it an attractive place to work. Luis says, "I love working at Il Vino to be honest. I love the job. You have fun while you work, you look at girls all night, I don't know, you are with your friends, the servers are nice. I love working there is the truth." However, as Luis learned himself, there is very little job security in the restaurant business. Saying that they wanted to cut personnel, the owners at Il Vino demoted Luis from a night busboy to a day busboy and he went from making over five hundred dollars a week to just two hundred and fifty. Since then, his motivation to work declined, as did his status at Il Vino. When he recently asked for a raise, he was dismissed by Tony, "There's the door, if you don't like it here." Discouraged, Luis started drinking and partying heavily on the weekends, a habit not conducive to his new 8:00 AM start time. After repeated warnings about arriving to work late, Luis was finally fired from Il Vino when he failed to show up for work two days in a row.

Job insecurity is intensified by the lack of benefits and pensions. This is a drawback that many restaurant workers share, not just the Mexican immigrant employees. Only one undocumented worker that I interviewed, Rene, receives health insurance—which was enough to lure him away from a higher paying construction job. Thus even though the Lions cite health insurance as a job characteristic that is important to them, it remains out of reach for all but a few.

Getting Paid and Managing Money

About half of the busboys' income is earned as cash tips. The distribution and allocation of tip income has its own set of rules, and being a tipped employee has important implications. On an average weekend night, there are three bartenders and between fifteen and seventeen servers ("server" is the gender-neutral term for waiters and waitresses) "on the floor" at Il Vino. While the busyness of the restaurant and the amount of tips that are earned can vary widely night to night and season to season, a good server can expect to make between one hundred and three hundred dollars in tips in a night. Each of the fifteen to seventeen servers and all three bartenders are expected to allocate at least fifteen percent of their tips to the busboys. This is called "tipping out." Let's say that on a typically busy Saturday night, the average tip income earned by the servers and bartenders is two hundred and fifty dollars. If there are fifteen servers and three bartenders who each make two hundred and fifty dollars, and they each tip out forty dollars (which is just over fifteen percent) to the busboys, the busboys as a group make seven-hundred and twenty dollars. Distributed evenly among five busboys, this amounts to a nightly cash income of one hundred and forty four dollars each.

On Friday and Saturday nights, the busboys generally earn between one hundred and one hundred and seventy dollars each in tips. Sunday through Thursday there is less business, less tips, but also fewer busboys. On these nights the two to three busboys who are on the floor will usually make between twenty dollars each (on very slow nights, like Mondays) and one hundred and fifty dollars each (on busier nights like Sunday and Thursday). There are, of course, nights that are unusually slow—for example, during a heavy snow storm—in which nobody makes much money. There are also nights in which the money pours in—like a Saturday night in the summer in which the dining room is packed and there are also large parties in the banquet rooms—and busboys can easily make upwards of two hundred dollars each. Il Vino doesn't get much of a lunch crowd, and daytime busboys earn very little in tips, between nothing and forty dollars or so.

It used to be common practice for servers to "side tip" busboys, or give a little extra cash to a particular busboy who did an exceptional job. The side tip was his to keep; he was not expected to share it with the other busboys. Official policy at Il Vino now discourages side tipping, since all of the busboys want to work with the servers who are more prone to side tip, but it still happens occasionally, particularly for banquet parties. The owners also occasionally give a bonus "side tip" to a favorite busboy, although this is more rare. The most striking example is when Rene returned from his honeymoon, and Tony handed him an envelope that contained enough cash to cover his honeymoon expenses—a bonus that amounted to over two thousand dollars.

All of the busboys work on Friday and Saturday nights and most work at least two other nights per week. Alberto, for example, works Sunday, Tuesday, Thursday, Friday, and Saturday nights. Rene works Thursday, Friday, and Saturday nights and Monday through Wednesday days. As I mentioned, it is difficult to estimate an exact annual income for a busboy since tip income varies nightly and seasonally. But in an average week, a busboy can earn upwards of three hundred dollars in tips—or more than fifteen thousand dollars per year in tips alone.

The Lions earn an hourly wage that is at or just over the regular minimum wage and receive a biweekly check from the payroll department for their first forty hours of work; they pay taxes on that income. At Uncle Luigi's, overtime pay is issued separately from another account without taxes and as straight pay—that is, workers do not receive time-and-a-half for overtime hours as required by law. Alejandro explained to me that, although it seems as though the busboys are being taken advantage of, this two-check system actually works in their favor. First, since no taxes are taken out of the overtime check, the net pay is actually very close to the amount it would be if it were issued at time-and-a-half after taxes. Second, since it does not cost Uncle Luigi's more to pay for overtime, the busboys are allowed to work more hours. That is, if Uncle Luigi's paid time-and-a-half for overtime, the managers would limit the busboys to forty hours per week. So with the two-check system, the busboys can all work more than forty hours per week, and this is a very important source of extra income for them.

Being tipped employees has important implications for both the busboys' approach to work and their attitudes about exploitation. In most capitalist industries (take manufacturing for example), there is a clear inverse relationship between how much workers can earn in wages and how much profit the company can make. For tipped employees, nearly the opposite is true: the more money the company makes, the more money the employee is likely to make. A fifteen percent tip on a one-hundred and fifty dollar check is more than fifteen percent of a one-hundred dollar check is more than fifteen percent of a fifty-dollar check. The more money guests spend on dinner, the more money they spend on tips. The goals of the boss and the worker are, if not exactly the same, at least overlapping. Having the busboys earn tips also diffuses the labor costs of the company, allowing Il Vino and Uncle Luigi's, for example, to retain highly competent busboys without compensating them more directly.

Many undocumented workers bolster their regular incomes with informal economic practices such as side jobs and bulk recycling. For example, Chuy, who works in construction during the day, collects scrap copper wire from job sites. Every month or so he sells the wire to a scrap metal place and can earn one hundred dollars or more for a box of the copper. He uses that money to buy himself shoes, clothes, and tools, which he often finds for discount prices at the local flea market. One undocumented Mexican family separates the garbage in Il Vino's dumpster, packing all of the recyclables into their van and taking them across the state line to Michigan where the recyclable materials can be sold for more money (up to 10 cents per bottle). Marta and Carlos are a married couple who work at Uncle Luigi's, she as a bathroom attendant and he as a cook. Once a month they clean the apartment building that one of the owners of Uncle Luigi's also owns. They are paid one hundred dollars in cash to spend an afternoon vacuuming and dusting the common areas of the building and maintaining the landscaping in the summer.

Almost all of the Lions regularly accept side jobs, or one-time jobs for which they are paid cash. Side jobs can range from moving, painting, and cleaning, to more skilled or dangerous jobs, such as construction projects, cleaning windows, and clearing trees. The going rate seems to be about one hundred dollars per worker for a day's work. Manuel, Luis, and Chuy, the Lions who are qualified to work in construction, often team up to accept side jobs. Between them, they can do framing, drywall, electricity, and trim work. They agree to do small-scale construction projects for far less than a homeowner would pay if they contracted union workers. Although they realize that they are underselling their labor, they defend this choice by pointing out that working cheaply is better than not working at all. Manuel says, "[A fellow construction worker] says I'm an idiot for doing the job so cheap, but I'd be a bigger idiot if I were sitting at home not doing anything." Most side jobs are found through word-of-mouth, and not just owners and coworkers, but even regular customers at Il Vino solicit busboys to do side jobs for them.

Undocumented Mexican immigrants also find ways to stretch their dollars. As I discuss in more detail later, all of the busboys live in households with three or more income earners, allowing them to disperse household expenses and absorb the risk of individual unemployment. Members of a household not only share bills and meals, but often cars as well. Both Alberto, who was a skilled mechanic in Mexico, and Chuy, who has some knowledge of cars, help fellow busboys keep their older cars running. When shopping, the workers choose discount stores like Marshalls and TJ Maxx, rather than the mall, for brand-name clothes.

Although the Lions are well paid relative to many other undocumented workers, even an annual income near the U.S. national average does not go very far. Not only do the Lions have to pay their own living expenses, but their incomes are diffused throughout their families. The single men, Leonardo, Roberto, Chuy, and Luis, send remittance money home to their parents, while Rene, Alberto, Lalo, and Manuel are the primary financial providers for multiple children. After the children are clothed and fed, the rent is paid, and unexpected costs are taken care of, there is often very little money left over. Among the Lions, financial security appears to diverge according to whether or not the worker has family in Mexico. The two men who support wives and children in Mexico—Alberto and Lalo—are the least financially secure. This is probably partly due to their higher household expenses and partly due to their tendency to work for temporary periods in the United States that are interspersed with trips home in which they do not work at all (in Alberto's case) or work for very low wages (in Lalo's case). The five men who have worked in the U.S. the longest—Alejandro, Chuy, Leonardo, Rene, and Roberto—are the most financially stable and are, in fact, very near the cusp of attaining middle class status.[4] It is notable that all five men are seriously involved with women who earn annual incomes that near or surpass their own—an important contribution to the men's security. In addition, Chuy, Leonardo, and Roberto do not support children and, although they do send remittances home to parents, they are able to save more money over the long term. Alejandro and Manuel have both experienced significant job changes over the past several years which have undermined their tenuous financial security. Although his wife works, Manuel reports that supporting three children in Chicago drains much of their household income; his family suffers recurring periods of instability. Alejandro supports one son but says that his inability to save enough money to buy his own home is mainly due to his spending habits—in particular, he enjoys taking his girlfriend out for nice dinners.

Utilizing a Social Network: Households

Mexican immigrant households often consist of multiple adult income-earners who are not all members of the same immediate family. The Institute for Latino Studies at Notre Dame recently reported that nearly one-third of Chicago-area Latino immigrants live in households with three or more income-earners, compared with only 8 percent of non-Latino households.[5] In addition, even though Latino immigrants have the lowest median incomes as individuals, Latino families are less likely to be poor and more likely to own their own home than other groups.[6] This suggests that the strategies that immigrant workers employ to combat financial insecurity extend beyond the job site and into the household. This section examines the intra-household strategies that make these extended household arrangements work, including how chores and living expenses are distributed, and how workers deal with conflict in households composed of multiple adult males.

The Lions' households are at once economic units in which the costs and duties of daily living are shared among household members, and social spaces in which housemates rely on each other for friendly interaction and emotional support. The migration chain that Alejandro established eventually brought over Rene's best friend from Mexico, then Rene himself and his brother Chuy, as well as Alejandro's two brothers, Alberto and Carlos, and Alberto's wife's brother, Luis. All of these men, and all of the Lions, have not only been working together but living together in various arrangements as well. These extended living arrangements have both advantages and disadvantages. They provide advantages in that they allow the Lions to disperse financial insecurity and household responsibilities, and, because they gather together friends from "back home," they provide emotional security and comfort for men who are separated from their families. But living as an adult man with other adult men in crowded conditions comes with challenges as well, including lack of privacy, messiness, noise, and conflict. The Lions have multiple, well-developed mechanisms for dealing with these challenges and maximizing the potential benefits of their rather large households.

Nearly twenty years after Alejandro arrived in Chicago alone, he once again lives with family. Alejandro, Alberto, Carlos, and Luis rent a small, white frame house in a Chicago suburb. Their house is a mid-century ranch that sits at the end of a neat, working-class block dominated by single-family homes. Their block dead-ends at freight-train tracks that crisscross Chicago's southwestern suburbs and also pass by Rene and Chuy's house just a few blocks away. The house is not beautiful, but it is in good condition. As the senior members of the house, Alejandro and Alberto each have their own bedroom, while Luis and Carlos share the third room. At any given time there might be a cousin or friend who is also spending the night on the couch until a good living situation of his own becomes available.

The décor is very "bachelor"—the living room is dominated by an enormous blue sectional sofa and a television. The younger men's bedroom has two twin mattresses on the floor, a TV, and an Xbox video game console, which the guys spend countless hours playing. Alberto and Alejandro's bedrooms are also rather bare. Alberto has a mattress on the floor, and a small TV with a built-in VCR player which sits atop one of two narrow dressers. Alejandro's bedroom is the most furnished of the three, as his bed actually sits on a bed frame and is pushed against a dark laminate head board. Alejandro has even hung a picture on the wall—a team photo of the Chivas, Guadalajara's soccer team.

Like all of the other Lions' households, this house is neat. Not just neat compared with dorm rooms or other apartments that I have seen in which single males live together, but really neat. It is clean; there are no dirty dishes in the sink or dust on the furniture. There are lots of dirty clothes, especially in Luis and Carlos' room, but even those are mostly confined to the one small closet. The men tell me that they share the household chores, which are completed on a daily basis, and conform to the chore schedule that is posted on the refrigerator door. They also share the household expenses. The monthly rent for their house is eight hundred dollars, which is split evenly among the four of them. As a household, they spend another sixty or so dollars a month on electricity, and between one hundred and two hundred for gas. Each household member thus spends around three hundred dollars a month for his total living expenses (not including food).

The brothers and Luis have lived together (on and off) for several years, and they get along well. Luis says that having a schedule of chores helps suppress conflict because every roommate knows what is expected of him. They respect each other's bedrooms and give each other as much privacy as possible. Luis also says that it's important to have a laid back attitude regarding noise and company. When fights do occur, they can often be attributed to someone having had too much to drink. The conflicting parties then avoid each other for a day or two until the hard feelings wear away.

Leonardo and Roberto share a two-bedroom apartment with two other men—Leonardo's older brother Juan, who also worked at Il Vino, and Gus, a busboy at another nearby restaurant; all four of the roommates are from León. The apartment building that they live in is owned by the owners of Uncle Luigi's, and about half of the apartments are rented to Uncle Luigi's employees. Mexican immigrants rent only two of the sixteen apartments in the building; the other tenants are mostly young white workers. Leonardo and Roberto's apartment is on the second floor and features a small balcony facing a courtyard. We sit out there to do interviews, talking above the rush of traffic coming from the nearby expressway.

This apartment is rather spare on furnishings, with only a small sofa, coffee table, and television in the common living area. Leonardo and his brother Juan sleep on mattresses in the bedroom that they share, while Roberto has somehow finagled the other bedroom to himself. Gus sleeps on the living room sofa but stores his clothes in the bedroom closet in Roberto's room. Like Alejandro and Alberto's house, this apartment is remarkably clean considering that four single men share it. Tacked to one of the walls in the living room is a sheet of notebook paper titled "*Quehaceres*," or "Chores." It is a schedule showing which roommate is responsible for doing the chores on each day of the week. These chores normally consist of picking up, sweeping, and wiping down the kitchen. Each roommate is responsible for washing his own dishes and the roommates take turns cleaning the bathroom once a week.

Household expenses are divided equally among the four roommates. The rent for this apartment is eight-hundred dollars a month, and the guys spend another hundred and fifty on utilities. This adds up to monthly living expenses of under two hundred and fifty dollars for each roommate.

Roberto and Leonardo have lived together for nearly four years, while Gus and Juan are more recent arrivals. The composition of roommates in this apartment has changed over the years. Alejandro, Rene, Chuy, and Manuel have all lived there, as have former Il Vino busboys who have returned to Mexico or otherwise moved on. Some of these former roommates were particularly fond of late-night drinking and loud music, and Rene explains that eventually his friends who like to "party" all night ended up in one apartment, while their more quiet and serious friends ended up in a neighboring apartment. Composing households in this way helps keep the peace and maintain the stability of living arrangements. When serious conflicts do occur, the household is likely to split up, with members of the feuding parties going their separate ways. Even those households that are consistently made up of Mexican immigrants change composition over the years, as workers leave for and arrive from Mexico, get married, or go off in search of better opportunity.

Rene is the only Lion who owns his own house. He lives with his wife, Molly, and their two children in a duplex that they bought together. Rene and Molly live on the first floor and rent out the two small apartments upstairs, one to Chuy and the other to another undocumented immigrant family. There is also a basement that at any given time is likely to be a temporary shelter for a newly arrived friend. The house is over one hundred years old and, though it is not elaborate, it has the original wood floors in some rooms and very high ceilings on the first floor. Rene and

Molly also have a beautiful yard that makes a lovely gathering spot for summer get-togethers. This house is the social center for the Lions. Except for Leonardo and Alberto (who work on Sundays) and Lalo (who they say is just too old to party), all of the friends gather here many Sundays when the weather is nice. Rene grills steak and chile peppers while Molly makes margaritas. A small boom box plays *rock-en-español* [Spanish-language rock] CDs, competing with the rumble of passing trains, the shrieks of playing children, and spirited conversations about everything from U.S. presidential politics to tire rims. There is a family atmosphere here that provides comfort to the workers. Molly says that Alberto often comes over during the day just to sit in the yard and pet Chuy's dog.

Chuy lives in a modest apartment on the second floor of the house. He is the only Lion who lives by himself, a privilege for which he pays $250 a month in rent. Although it is small, the apartment is quite nice, with original wood floors and tiles. Chuy values the privacy and tranquility that living alone affords him, but he also makes frequent visits downstairs to play with his niece and nephew and to enjoy his sister-in-law's cooking. While Chuy has no roommates, he has constant company in his dog, Laica, a midnight-black mutt.

Lalo, Omar, and Manuel live with in-law relatives. Lalo lives with his sister-in-law, her husband, their son, and his own son in a house on the south side of Chicago. Manuel lives with his wife, Liliana, their two sons, her parents, and her three sisters in a two-story house in suburban Chicago. This living situation is very difficult for Manuel and Liliana. She feels caught between her parents and her husband, who often have very different ideas about how to raise the children. He feels like he's lost his privacy and independence. Manuel's goal is to move his family into their own apartment, but recently his employment has been erratic. He left Il Vino in 2005 for a better paying job in construction, but when the construction industry was hit hard by the contracting economy in 2008, Manuel lost his job. He has been earning some money doing informal side jobs, but, until he can find steady work, Manuel and his family will remain with his in-laws.

For all of the Lions, transnational work-life is made bearable by the love and support of their family and friends. For most of these men, there will be a permanent emotional connection to both Mexico and the U.S., as they will always have family in both places. Without a major overhaul of immigration policy, few of the Lions will be able to travel between the U.S. and Mexico with any frequency. Instead, they will continue to cultivate co-immigrant communities and households in the U.S. to provide them with vital material and non-material resources.

Notes

1. See also Valenzuela, Jr., et al. 2006; Ready and Brown-Gort 2005.
2. See also Garcia 2005.
3. See also Adler 2005; Pribilsky 2007.
4. See Epilogue.
5. Ready and Brown-Gort 2005.
6. Ready and Brown-Gort 2005.

CHAPTER FIVE

Echándole Ganas
Working Hard

A LITTLE EXTRA: ROBERTO

I came to the U.S. to hang out with white people. No, I'm kidding! Look, the first time I came I was sixteen and I just wanted to see the U.S., and so after a while I went back to Mexico. The second time I came I had a stronger purpose; I wanted to earn some money to see what I could do. I got a job at Uncle Luigi's with Alejandro, and that's where I met everyone from León. Most people who come here from Mexico are from the rural areas, the country, they work on the land. But we are from the city, so there aren't as many of us, you know?

When I first got here, I worked as a dishwasher eight or nine hours a day, six days a week. And they were paying me four-fifty, five dollars an hour [in 1997]. And I was like, oh man, this is crazy. It was a different country, a different language, and you're like, man, what the fuck? You don't know what to do, you don't know what's up. It takes you a while to adapt to the job, to whatever job, it takes a while. But with time, when you're with other Mexicans, they help you because they speak the same language as you. And it depends on you, too, if you want to do well in the job, mentally and physically. And I have worked food prep, busboy, construction, now I'm working as a busboy again, making good money, thank god, and working hard [*echándole ganas*].

Our job is as a busboy, right, but we also do construction, organizing, throwing stuff out, cleaning, so it's a little extra that the boss notices. So it benefits the job, the company, the restaurant, and it benefits us. And they save money, because they don't have to pay people to— you know, they want to take down this wall and we do it for them. They don't have to pay people to do it. But the other side of it is that it benefits us too, you know? In money, in more hours. Those are benefits. We're not going to come to work and say, no, that's not my job. What do you think they'd say? "Well, do you want to work or not?" But like I said, they know we'll never tell them no. If you're my boss and you tell me, "You know what, cut the lawn, arrange the flowers, all that," I'll do it for you. And I'll do a good job and moreover I'll do a little extra so that, "Wow!" You come back and "Oh, you surprised me!" You start to win the boss over in the sense that you put effort into the job and after a while he's going to give you more money.

We've been doing this job for a long time and we know the job well. And the bosses know that we know the job, that's why they come and ask us, "Do you think it will be busy this weekend?" They ask our opinion. "Hey, what about this? What do you think about this? Is this good here?" "No, you should change this." "Oh, yeah? Okay, change it." You know, they pay attention to what we say. At Il Vino they know that we know the job well, that's why they ask us what we think.

I think that at work it's always important to be in a good mood. It's contagious. Work is work, right, so if you come to work and you're having problems with someone and you're sad or pissed off, what do the other guys do? You come and everyone is like, "Hey man, what's up?" The other guy is in a good mood, "What's up man?" It makes you laugh even when you don't want to. You say what's up and everything is cool. So being in a good mood is contagious and when everyone is chatting together the time goes by faster. I think that's one of the main things that you have to do, that people have to do at work. Laughter is health [*la risa es salud*] and so it's better to be laughing.

When you work as a team, the job gets done better and faster, and you don't have to kill yourself as much. When we work as a team, we all work together as though we were a motor and the cylinders are, "toom, toom, toom." But if just one is kind of fucked up, now you have to work more, and it's not fair that one guy is like that. And the complaints start, "Hey man, what the fuck?" Like for example if tomorrow is going to be really busy, "Okay, you do this, you do this, I'll do this, you do this." And that's how we do it and everyone is equal. And it's cool, let's get to work. It's not just one person, no one person is going to come and say, "Okay, I want...." No. Everyone is equal, we discuss it, "Yeah, okay, what do you think?" "How about this?" Like that, "Cool, let's get to work." And we eat our Wheaties and we all work really hard.

On weekend nights, when Il Vino is busy and the lounge is crowded with diners waiting for a table, five busboys get together to stock the bar. I call this "the Busboy Show." First, the busboys load about twenty cases of beer and two bins of liquor onto a wheeled cart. Then they push this cart through the restaurant up to the service station at the bar. Two or three of them will stay on the outside of the bar with the cart and the other two or three will go behind the bar. The bartenders and servers get out of the way. Like a sped-up assembly line, one busboy will snatch a case of beer from the cart and throw it—literally, throw it in the air—to a second busboy standing closer to the bar. This busboy catches it easily and tosses it across the top of the bar, where a busboy standing behind the bar grabs it and throws it to a fourth busboy, who catches it and stacks it in front of the beer coolers. A final busboy will rip open the cases and stock beer in the coolers. They work lightning-quick—it only takes them about a minute to empty the cart. Customers and restaurant employees gather around to watch, commenting on the busboys' strength and speed. The busboys enjoy the attention and ham it up for onlookers, prodding each other to go faster and faster. They also try to outdo one another by throwing the cases as high into the air as they can. Sometimes, when there's a new busboy, the other guys will throw him an empty case just to laugh as he juggles it in the air.

There is universal agreement at Il Vino that the Mexican immigrant busboys are the best workers at the restaurant—an association of Mexican immigrants and hard work that is not unique to Il Vino. In fact, the conception of Mexican immigrants as a laboring class has a long history in the United States, and for more than a century Mexican workers have often been considered a diligent, tractable segment of the U.S. workforce.[1] Ethnographic research shows that the perception of Mexican immigrants as hard workers continues to have popular currency.[2] In particular, many low-wage employers express their approval of Mexican immigrants' apparent willingness to do low-wage, low-status work.[3] But where does this apparent willingness to work hard come from? And why would presumably permanent members of the low-wage labor force put so much effort into being hard workers?

Mexican immigrants' work ethic is often attributed to their "culture" or "cultural background."[4] Not only coworkers and managers at restaurants like Il Vino, but also my colleagues at the university have suggested that Mexican immigrants' work ethic "may be just cultural." This use of "culture" implies that there is something integral to Mexican society that causes Mexican people to be hard workers, an idea that is widely promoted by management at Il Vino. For example, the general manager says, "They are just phenomenal workers. I don't know what it's like in Mexico, but something happens there. Something is instilled in them from birth I think." To be sure, lots of workers in Mexico do work very hard, but the idea that Mexicans are already and always hard workers—and that hard work is due to Mexican culture—glosses over variation among Mexican workers, ignores the role of inequality in structuring work conditions, and diminishes workers' agency on the job.[5] When it is applied to immigrants, the idea that Mexicans are naturally hard workers overlooks the historical subordination of Mexican workers in the United States, which has given rise to an association of Mexican immigrants and a "willingness" to work hard. For example, Mexican workers in the U.S. are not only typically funneled into low-wage, low-status jobs, but frequently relegated to piece-rate work, temporary contract labor, or non-unionized employment in which income and job security are directly tied to the degree of "hard work" that a worker can put forth. In the end, the notion that working hard is attributable to "Mexican culture" naturalizes Mexican immigrants' subordination and reduces their work performances to a putative cultural inclination for socially degraded, back-breaking labor.[6]

The Lions are well aware that they are considered very hard workers, and they turn this reputation to their advantage, reproducing stereotypes of themselves as hard workers and making themselves indispensable on the job. For example, when these workers throw cases of beer to each other (instead of simply and less spectacularly handing them off), they are achieving at least four interrelated effects. First, they are exerting control over how they are perceived by their American bosses, coworkers, and customers. This form of "impression management" (Goffman 1959) taps into U.S. folk culture notions of "Mexican work ethic," reinforcing an association of the Mexican staff with hard work and enhancing their job security at the restaurant. Second, they are cultivating norms of hard work amongst themselves, effectively creating a culture of work that shapes how each busboy approaches his work and perceives his labor. Third, they are responding to particular structural vulnerabilities—financial insecurity, racialization, and social stigmatization—and attempting to manage and reduce these vulnerabilities. Fourth, reproducing racialized stereotypes of "Mexican work ethic" can have the ultimate effect of reinforcing racial circumscription of the Mexican immigrant staff, an unintended but important outcome.

But the Mexican immigrant busboys at Il Vino—whose core members are also Lions—are not always and already willing to work hard. In fact, they actively and continuously negotiate norms of hard work on the job, and new workers undergo a rigorous socialization process in which they learn to satisfy group expectations. This chapter explores how and why a willingness to work hard is cultivated by undocumented workers on the restaurant floor at Il Vino.

Extra Work, Flexible Work

A Hypothetical Day in the Work Life of an Il Vino Busboy

For Roberto, the work week begins in earnest on Thursday afternoon. His day off is Wednesday, which he usually spends running errands and relaxing with his girlfriend. Thursday morning, Roberto is up and running, briefly straightening the apartment before heading off to the neighborhood gym. He tries to get in at least an hour and a half workout, which he divides between a cardio routine and weight lifting. Afterward, he grabs lunch, a salad or sandwich, then heads back home to clean up, iron his uniform, and rest before going to work.

On Thursdays, Roberto and Rene are the first busboys to arrive at Il Vino and are usually clocked in by two thirty in the afternoon. Even though Thursdays are less busy than Fridays or Saturdays, it is a hectic night for the three busboys, Roberto, Rene, and Leonardo, who are responsible for maintaining the floor and setting up for the Friday rush. When Rene and Roberto arrive on Thursday afternoon, the first thing that they do is get the reservation book and floor plan from the hostess desk. From the storage room in the back of the restaurant, Rene and Roberto chart their day. First, they make sure the dining room is clean for the dinner rush and that the server stations are stocked; they bring fresh bottles of condiments and extra shakers for salt and pepper from dry storage. They cut lemons for water and set them next to water pitchers, which they get from the dish room. They spot vacuum the floor. If there are a lot of reservations or parties, they open new boxes of silverware and bring them to the dishwasher to be cleaned. Then, they check with the bartender and get a liquor and glassware order; wine glasses may need to be brought up from dry storage. They stock the bar with beer and wine. Next they make an "86" list of all out-of-stock menu items to give to the bartenders and servers. Then, they get bags of clean linens from storage, open them, and set them in the server stations for easy reach later.

Finally, they check with servers to see if they need anything, empty the garbage cans, and check bathrooms for paper supplies and soap; while there, they wipe down the counters and spot sweep the bathroom floors. Around four o'clock, Leonardo clocks in and joins the effort.

At some point during preparation, a large party arrives without a reservation. The busboys' walkie-talkies rattle, "Hey guys? We have a party of twelve in section two." Roberto responds, "Okay, I got it." The busboys drop what they're doing and converge on section two, pulling out chairs and pushing tables together. Once the tables are properly arranged and set with napkins, silverware, and side plates, Roberto and Leonardo go back to their preparations and Rene brings twelve glasses of water and three loaves of hot bread to the seated party. An hour later, the dinner rush starts in earnest. From six o'clock to nine-thirty, the busboys don't stop moving. They are filling waters, serving bread, carrying out food orders, clearing plates, boxing leftovers, refilling coffee, bringing wine and ice to the bar, emptying garbages, and turning over tables. Finally, around ten o'clock, the rush dies down, and the busboys' second shift begins.

Leonardo continues to work the floor, while Rene and Roberto start to prepare the banquet rooms for the next day. They study the reservation sheets, noting whether they need to bring out long tables or round tables and how many, the kind and quantity of table linens, the number of chairs, the color of the napkins, and, if the party is banquet-style, the quantity and type of chafing dishes. Setting up the banquet rooms can take an hour or more, as the busboys are continually interrupted to get supplies for the stations, bring out an order for a busy server, empty garbages, or check the bathrooms. Rene is called behind the bar for a half-hour, to help the bartender catch up with the servers' drink orders. As the restaurant empties out, the busboys replenish all of the silverware, linens, and condiments that were used during the shift, and they clean. They clean everything, flipping all of the chairs on top of the tables to sweep the floor, wiping down countertops, doors, and ledges; they even dust the piano. Sometime well after midnight, after all the staff except for the closing server and manager have left for the evening, Leonardo grabs three Coronas from the bar and Rene brings out a plate of cold calamari that he cajoled from his friends in the kitchen. The guys sit down for the first time since they arrived and count their tips.

Mexican immigrants who work in food and beverage service are typically segregated into the lowest-paid jobs as busboys, line cooks, and dishwashers.[7] Even though these jobs are socially degraded, a willingness to be diligent and tractable is expected from immigrant workers in these positions; it is an essential feature of their labor. Alejandro explains that, as a busboy, "Most of the employers will tell you straight out, 'You're going to do what we ask you to do.' They'll say to you, 'You're going to be a busboy but if I call you and ask you to do this, you're going to do it.'" Indeed, the managers at Il Vino demand flexibility from the bus staff. The general manager says, "I mean, it's not really a busboy's job to clean up vomit off the floor, but...I think that we just look at them as busboys and they will do really whatever you ask them to do. From garbages to cleaning out toilets to—you know. So I think we're harder on them in that we take it for granted...and expect that they will do whatever we ask them to do." This sentiment is echoed by other supervisors at restaurants in Chicago, who identify Mexican immigrants' willingness to do "whatever we ask" as an important component of their labor. Whether a customer locks his keys in his car, the owner's mother needs a ride somewhere, or someone has made a mess in the bathroom, the busboys invariably take care of it. The busboys are called on to do all tasks that do not fit into anyone else's job description, and the more unattractive the task is to other workers at Il Vino, the more likely that it will fall to the busboys. As Lalo says with a hint of humor, "For us, everything is our job."

Doing extra work has become part of the everyday routine for the Mexican immigrant busboys at Il Vino, resulting in an increased and diversified workload. They routinely work twelve hours straight, sometimes leaving only to be back at work a few hours later. But working long hours and keeping up with the workload is only the beginning of being an Il Vino busboy; Il Vino busboys not only have stamina, they have talent. They pride themselves on anticipating the needs of customers and servers and on having things ready before they are asked. They are excellent busboys, but they also know how to bartend and can wait tables themselves in a pinch. They lift heavy food trays high above their heads, often one in each hand, and deftly maneuver through crowds. They expertly balance full trays of glasses of water and almost never spill (and if they do, they will never hear the end of it from their friends). The busboys can carry three cases of beer on their shoulder and wind their way from the back of the restaurant to the bar without bumping into a single customer or employee. (See Figure 5.1.)

The busboys at Il Vino have not always had such a heavy workload. Over the years, they have slowly taken over responsibility for more and

FIGURE 5.1 Leonardo carries three cases of beer to the bar on his shoulder. (*Courtesy of the author*)

more tasks. For example, in the past the waitstaff at Il Vino helped clean by vacuuming their sections and wiping down the server stations after the restaurant closed. But the busboys say that the servers did such a half-hearted cleaning job that they, the busboys, would have to clean up after them and, over time, the waitstaff's cleaning chores became the busboys' responsibility. Roberto explains his frustration: "Sometimes there are things [that need to be done] and it's not that you don't have anything else to do, it's who's going to do it? They're not going to do it. So there was a time when we just started saying, 'I'll do it, I'll do it, I'll do it.' And that's how it stayed. It's still that way.... Now we have to do it. If we don't, there'll be problems for us." What starts out as "extra" work can easily slide over into the busboys' area of responsibility, resulting in an ever-expanding definition of their job description.

Sometimes the busboys look for extra work to do to stay busy during slow periods. Once, during a slow lunch shift, Rene decided to clean the bottoms of all of the chairs in the unused parts of the restaurant (only the front section of the restaurant opens for lunch). Table by table, the busboys flipped the chairs upside down and wiped down the legs with soapy water. If there was gum or other unidentified gunk on the bottom of the chairs, they used razors to scrape it off. On another slow day, Rene and Alberto cleaned the alley and the back walls of the building with a power-washer, then climbed extension ladders to dust the wood beams and fans attached to the ceiling. The busboys explain that keeping busy not only makes the day go by faster, but helps ensure that their hours do not get cut during slow periods. In fact, management's most common complaint about the bus staff is that they "milk the schedule" by keeping more busboys working than are really necessary.

When Il Vino first opened and every night was busy, the busboys' work was necessarily more confined to the narrow definition of what a busboy's job includes. As business has slowed down, there has been increasing pressure for busboys to do more varied work, in fewer hours, and often with fewer workers. By diversifying the tasks that busboys perform, Colleen and Tony avoid having to hire other workers to do things like maintenance, cleaning, landscaping, and painting. Since the owners have mostly refused to hire additional workers, all of this extra work is absorbed by the existing busboy staff, resulting in a much heavier workload for them. At one meeting with the busboy staff in the winter of 2007, the general manager justified the busboys' intensified workload by explaining to them that they actually had two distinct jobs. One is to support the service staff (busboy narrowly defined), for which they earn tips. Their other job is to "work for the owners," for which they earn an hourly rate at or just over the minimum wage. The manager told the busboys that, if they did not want to do the extra work, he would pay them "server wages," the amount that waiters and bartenders make (at the time just over $4 per hour) instead of regular wages ($7.50 per hour). By identifying extra work as the justification for the busboys' wages, management instituted "extra" work as part of the busboys' regular responsibilities. By asserting that any busboy who doesn't want to do it can choose not to and be paid a reduced wage, management gives the appearance that extra work is voluntary, heading off charges of exploitation.

The ever-expanding list of busboys' responsibilities is taking its toll on the workers. Some of the busboys either have other jobs in the morning or children that they help get off to school, resulting in regular sleep deprivation. The nighttime busboys also feel frustrated at what they see as poor management decisions that result in too much work for them and not enough work for the daytime busboys. Although many nighttime busboys also work during the day, in the past there has been conflict between the two groups because the nighttime busboys felt that they did a disproportionate amount of work, and the daytime busboys begrudged the fact that the nighttime guys made more money. The busboys also dislike inefficient or disorganized servers who cause them more work. Even though they appreciate the value that comes with having a lot of responsibility, the busboys also resent the caprice with which work is heaped onto their shoulders.

While being asked to take on extra work is a source of complaint when workers are talking amongst themselves, there is universal agreement that complaining to management should be avoided. In fact, the busboys often respond promptly and with energy, if not enthusiasm, when called on to do extra tasks. They demonstrate their "willingness to work" by performing extra work without complaint and with alacrity. The workers even have a name for this performance—*echándole ganas*—which literally means "putting desire in it," but can be roughly translated as "putting effort into it," or "putting your back into it." But echándole ganas does not always come easy for workers, and the busboys continuously negotiate and enforce norms of hard work on the restaurant floor.

Learning the Ropes: Humor and Hazing

Even when Mexican immigrants come to the U.S. prepared to work hard, they still must be socialized into the work culture of their U.S. jobs. At Il Vino, most new busboys, including brothers, cousins, and childhood friends of the Lions, have a hard time keeping up with the pace and expectations of the job. Even those Lions who have worked at Il Vino for many years must be resocialized to work hard after extended vacations in Mexico. The core group of Il Vino busboys (Rene, Roberto, Leonardo, Chuy, and Alberto) who have worked there for many years negotiate expectations of their labor through their interactions with each other and with their coworkers and managers. These norms, in turn, regulate the labor of all Il Vino busboys.

When a busboy is hired at Il Vino, the first thing that happens is he gets a nickname. Every Lion has an unflattering nickname: Dumbo, Unibrow, Flower, even Manuel's kids are called *los bastarditos*, or "the little bastards." When a new busboy starts at Il Vino, he is likely to be working hard, trying to get along, when suddenly he finds that the other guys are laughing at him. They have probably decided that he looks like some cartoon character, or maybe a monkey or giraffe, and maybe they have even posted a picture of the character on the wall in the storage room with the new worker's name written on it. When Frank, a young white man, began working as a busboy several years ago, the other guys decided that his rather big belly reminded them of Homer Simpson and Frank became "Homero." One particularly messy busboy was briefly nicknamed "Katrina," after Hurricane Katrina, the storm that devastated the U.S. Gulf Coast in 2005. As soon as he understood the joke, "Katrina" made more of an effort to keep his tables neat, and the busboys found something else to tease him about. Arturo, a Mexican man in his mid-thirties who worked at Il Vino for two years, moved a bit slower than the other busboys, so the guys sarcastically called him "Ferrari." When they wanted him to move faster, the busboys would call Arturo over their walkie-talkies, "Hey Ferrari, vroom, vroom, vroooooom!" The trick for any new busboy is to be good-natured about the teasing, as any show of anger or hurt feelings will only result in more—and more unflattering—teasing. The busboys also have nicknames for most of the servers, and, in case you are wondering, I am "*la Ruda*" (the rough or aggressive one), a play on my name and an unfortunate comment on my interviewing style.

This use of humor is not all fun and games. Teasing is a critical part of the hazing process in which new busboys are socialized to be hard workers. The busboys agree that working together at the same level of intensity is important, and they use teasing to pressure each other into working hard in a nonconfrontational way. For their part, new busboys who must be taught the ropes count on the more established busboys to show them how to work. Luis explains: "Among the Mexicans we tell each other [to work better], right?...We trust each other to say, 'Look man, work harder, pick it up, okay?'...It's very important to us that someone helps you, tells you to work harder, or supports you." Busboys even receive instructions on informal work practices, like "looking like you want to work" by always walking quickly and responding to requests with enthusiasm. This socialization process establishes work norms and weeds out busboys who are not motivated to work hard or do not want to work as part of the team.

Much of the busboys' socialization takes place during the course of work via walkie-talkie radios. The busboys at Il Vino use walkie-talkies with earpieces to pass information, instructions, and requests to each other while they mind their respective sections of the restaurant. Managers can also tune in to the busboys' radio frequency to ask them for things. When the restaurant is busy, these radios can be extremely useful for keeping the work flow seamless and efficient. For example, a manager may come on the radio to ask the busboys to empty the garbage in the women's bathroom. One of the busboys, usually whoever is least busy or whose section is nearest the bathroom, will answer with an "I got it." The rest of the busboys then know who is going to empty the garbage and they will take care of his section for him. While he is emptying the garbage in the women's bathroom, the busboy is also likely to check the men's room garbage and the kitchen garbage cans, saving him from having to empty those later. In addition, since he will have to empty the garbage cans in the back of the restaurant near the storage rooms, another busboy may come on the radio and ask him for a favor: "While you're back there, I need two bottles of house Merlot for the bar." If it is likely to be a busy night, the busboy may grab four bottles of Merlot and two extra bottles of Cabernet, knowing that the lounge busboy will probably need them at some point in the night.

When the restaurant is not busy, early and very late in the night, the walkie-talkies serve a more light-hearted purpose, allowing the busboys to keep up a constant joking banter. The busboys take turns being the butt of each other's jokes, and even joking is often termed in the language of work. For example, a lot of chitchat over the radios is likely to provoke a playful, "Is that all you guys do, is joke around? Why don't you get some work done?" from another busboy. Or if a busboy is particularly busy the other guys might tease him, "Hurry up! Hurry up! Your waiters are calling for you! You better step on it!" Or a busboy might be interrupted during his dinner break by a frantic "Hey, where are you? The boss is looking for you!" only to find that the caller was playing a practical joke on him. If a busboy's section appears dirty, or if a table needs water, another busboy might come to help him and say to the server, "Where's your busboy? You don't have a busboy tonight or what?" Through joking, the busboys not only reinforce expectations of work, they also subtly discourage any tendencies toward self-aggrandizement or individuality. An over-eager busboy who asks "Hey, do you guys need anything? I'm not busy" might be answered with, "No, and don't be such a kiss-ass."

Sometimes play simply provides diversion and release after a hard day's work. One Saturday, as the busboys were cleaning after the restaurant closed, I noticed that Roberto had black hash marks swiped on both cheeks, like an NFL player or a guerrilla warrior. Then Rene walked by with a big, black hand-print on the back of his bald head. Later, I saw Chuy with the same black stuff smeared on his white undershirt. It turned out that Chuy had swiped the inside of a motorcycle exhaust pipe with his fingers, blackening his hands with the soot in the pipe. He swatted Rene on the back of the head and wiped his fingers on Roberto's cheeks, then ran away from them, giggling. Rene and Roberto quickly discovered the source of the soot and exacted their revenge. Practical joking and playing are an important part of the busboys' interactions and are a welcome distraction from the stresses of work. If they sit down to eat together before they start work, Rene might squirt ketchup in Roberto's seat, then Roberto is likely to return the favor by wiping the ketchup on Rene's ear. Once Roberto sprayed Leonardo in the face with a strong floral perfume; Leonardo got hold of the bottle and pretty soon the entire busboy staff stank like cheap feminine perfume. Playing at work not only provides a welcome distraction from the drudgeries of repetitive work, but strengthens the workers' social bonds as well. These bonds are crucial for creating and maintaining norms of teamwork.

Working as a Team

All of the immigrant busboys who work at Il Vino generally agree that having a team-oriented approach to work is the best quality that a busboy can have, while the worst busboys are those who act individualistically or are bossy. Alberto explains that, "It's important to work as a group because if you work in a group, you and your friends, the work is easier. When we do things together or help each other it's not so hard. Like if he needs something and it's far away and you're back there, 'I'll get it for you.' So, yeah, it's important to work together or as a team. It's much better." Not only does teamwork make the busboys faster and more efficient, it diffuses stress and insulates individual group members by spreading responsibility and accountability throughout the group. The group-oriented organization of work for busboys at Il Vino is encouraged by several factors, which I turn to briefly.

First, the busboys are treated as a group by management. Management will rarely directly reproach a busboy who they think is not doing a good job. Instead, they reprimand the busboys who have worked at Il Vino for the longest time, effectively making the more senior busboys responsible for the job performance of all busboys. The general manager says,

> There isn't really a direct manager [of the busboys], so it's amongst themselves. And I think that even as far as ownership goes, every

time there's a problem they go to an experienced busboy and say, "Can you take care of this?" I've seen that a million times. [The owners go to] Rene, Leonardo, sometimes Chuy, but mostly Rene and Leonardo. Maybe they look at them as the boss, but they'll make them go say, "Shit or get off the pot" [to a weak busboy].

Being held responsible for the performance of the group encourages the more senior busboys to take an active, group-oriented approach to directing work flow.

Also, working as a group improves job performance for the group as a whole and for each worker, making everyone's job easier and more pleasant. The busboys acknowledge that no one of them always feels like working hard; rather, it is their performance as a group that accomplishes the work well, quickly, and consistently. Working cooperatively allows the workers to have an occasional bad day because they know that their friends will help pick up their slack. Alejandro says, "If you know that somebody got your back, then you do something for them. You learn who you can count on and who you cannot…if you don't feel like working you could call somebody last minute and they would go and cover you." Having friends that you can count on helps relieve some of the pressure associated with long hours of stressful, repetitive work.

The system of tip distribution also encourages teamwork among the busboys. The servers at Il Vino put fifteen percent of their tips in a locked box at the end of each night. When the busboys finish cleaning, they retrieve the tip money and divide it into equal shares. This encourages teamwork because their tip income is based on collective effort; thus it is in each busboy's interest to make sure the others do well. The system of tip distribution also gives busboys leverage to apply pressure on those who they feel are not doing their share, and the busboys frequently assert that they are "not here to earn someone else's money."

Finally, established network and social ties among busboys facilitates a group orientation. All of the busboys come from the same hometown in Mexico. Several are related and have friendship ties that extend from nearly a decade to a lifetime. They mostly like and trust each other; this makes it easier for them to work as a team.

As vital as teamwork is for the busboys, it is not enough to simply work together. Busboys must conform to norms of equality and reciprocity in their work relations with each other. The significance of equality and helpfulness among the busboys is demonstrated by the distribution of leadership among the group and by the active suppression of boss-like behaviors. Even when one busboy is a nominal head busboy, he should be careful to work as hard as the others and not act bossy. This quote from Lalo shows how the busboys view Roberto's management style: "The leader that I have now [Roberto], the Mexican, he'll say to me, 'This is what we have to do for tomorrow. When you have time, see about this. When we're not busy, when the work has died down, we'll come and help you.' And he helps you and that's how it is." It is imperative that busboys in leadership positions continue to work as hard as the other workers because, if they do not, they can easily lose the respect and cooperation of the group.

In fact, many busboys who have been named head busboy were fired or demoted not long after their promotion. This is because promotion to a managerial position can disrupt the cohesion of the group and exclude the promoted busboy from the group's insulation. This happened to Leonardo, whose story is presented in the next section of this chapter, and to a young white worker named Frank, whose story appears in the next chapter. Rene and Roberto, who reject being in a formal position of authority, have been able to walk a fine line between appeasing the managers and avoiding the appearance of being a boss among their friends. In fact, Rene's strategy as manager is to "manage" as little as possible and to lead by example, often picking up slack himself. Because of the team orientation of the work group, Rene can count on his fellow busboys to help him. He says, "When me and Chuy work together I would tell him, 'Look, you do this and I'm going to do that.' He would say, 'Yeah, that's cool, I'll do it.' The guys from the apartment, Juan, Leonardo, and Roberto would come by, 'What are you doing? I'll help you.' And it was faster that way." By adopting a management strategy in which he picks up other workers' slack, Rene may add to his own workload, but he also reaffirms the stability of the group and puts subtle moral pressure on his fellow busboys to work harder as well.

Covering and Criticizing: Protecting the Group and Enforcing the Norms

In spite of the light-hearted nature of the busboys' banter, social acceptance in this work group depends on adherence to standards of work, and those who are not considered good workers can become alienated. Alejandro explains how this works at Uncle Luigi's:

> Say if you're in charge of the waters and you see an empty table and you're like "Oh, I'm in charge of the waters, I don't do that," I don't like that. If you have the free time, you go and do it. The same thing, you probably go to the bathroom and a table walks in, then somebody else will do the waters. And when people don't do that, the

other workers will come and say, "He's not, he doesn't want to do this, he's lazy, we always have to look for him when we need him, etcetera."

When a member of the work group is having a bad day, is unreliable, or in general does not work at the same high level as the others, the busboys have various mechanisms for protecting the group and enforcing the norms. When a busboy who is esteemed by the group is not contributing his share, the other workers will cover for him. Occasionally, a busboy may come to work intoxicated or upset and the other busboys will take over his section and send him home for the day. If the busboys pitch in and cover his section adequately, management may not even notice that they are missing a worker. Rene explains how they would try to protect a former busboy who got drunk and missed work: "I would tell [the bosses], 'He's sick, he's that,' but I was just lying.... I never said anything because in any case we all did his work among us. We all made the same and that was that." In fact, by covering for each other, the busboys can wield a considerable amount of influence in determining whether a busboy keeps his job or is fired. For example, Lalo moves more slowly than the other guys and has been on the managers' chopping block on more than one occasion. But the other busboys earnestly defend Lalo, telling management how helpful he is to them, and he has never been fired. While covering has the direct advantage of keeping management from interfering with the group, it is also a preferred strategy to "bossing" a fellow coworker because it protects the parity and social stability of the team.

When a worker has lost the esteem of the group by being a chronic drag on his coworkers or by failing to demonstrate the same level of energy and enthusiasm as the others, resentment can develop. The busboys usually deal with this by increasing levels of peer pressure. When the restaurant is busy, the senior busboys will cover for the slow worker to keep management from noticing weakness in the work group. But when they are cleaning or setting up, the busboys may slow down their own work, or even stop working entirely, until the slow worker catches up. This puts serious pressure on the weak busboy. If the situation still doesn't improve, a sit-down discussion with the slacking worker may be in order. Luis explains that, "Look, there is a time and place to say something. Like when we stay and have a drink after work, we'll tell him, 'Listen man, you suck, you sucked tonight. Try to do better.' And among the Mexicans we tell each other, right?" In extreme cases, the busboys will stop covering for a slacking worker and allow his weakness to be exposed to management; this usually results in the weak busboy's dismissal. This is a last resort however, and the workers prefer strategies that do not expose themselves to interference by management or risk the cohesion of their team.

The following case provides an example of how the busboys use teasing and peer pressure to enforce normative work behaviors, but will eventually withdraw their protection of a slacking coworker. When Leonardo started at Il Vino, he did double duty, working as a busboy and dishwasher during the day and cleaning at night. Leonardo proved himself to be a hard worker and was finally promoted to a night busboy, where he worked as a solid member of the group for four years. Leonardo was well-liked and well-respected by the other busboys, as well as by the waitstaff and management at Il Vino. Then he got promoted to head busboy and everything changed.

The head busboy does not get paid more than the other busboys, nor does he attend manager meetings like all of the other managers do; his job is basically to translate directions from management to the bus staff and keep any wayward busboys in line. Rene, who has seniority, is often the preferred head busboy but does not like being formally in charge. So when the management staff decided that they wanted to have a formal head busboy in the spring of 2008, Rene declined the position and Roberto was in Mexico. It was Leonardo's turn.

As soon as Leonardo was granted nominal management status, his work habits changed, as did his attitude toward working as part of a group. He began spending more and more time on the phone with his new girlfriend and would ask the other busboys to cover his section for him. At times he would disappear from work for an hour or more. Since Leonardo was a long-standing and valued member of the group, at first the other busboys covered for him and only chided him mildly for his behavior. But instead of going back to normal, Leonardo's conduct got more and more intolerable. He started ordering other busboys to do his work, even calling them his *gatos* (literally "cats," or "car jacks" but in this context it means "chumps"). Luis complained, "He spends the night talking on the phone to his girl and tells us, 'Gatos, gatos, I need this, gatos help me do this and this and this.'" The waiters and waitresses in Leonardo's section started to notice his long absences and complained to the other busboys about him. As they split tips and drank beer at the end of the night, the other busboys would try to talk to Leonardo about his behavior. Luis says, "When he got really bad, we would tell him, 'Look man, cut it out, you're going too far, okay? Why are you on the phone all night and you don't help out?'"

Leonardo's work habits still did not improve, and gradually—after several months—the other busboys started refusing to do his work for him. They stopped checking on his section and would only help when a member of the waitstaff asked them directly. Without the insulation and protection of the group, Leonardo's erratic work behavior called the attention of the general manager, who immediately demoted him and put him on the lunch shift, where he made very little in tips. Leonardo's work habits had been slipping for months, but it was not until the other busboys withdrew their protection of him that the managers became aware of his weaknesses. Chastened, Leonardo had to prove himself all over again, and it took him a year to get back in the other busboys' good graces and to re-earn his place as a nighttime busboy. This case not only illustrates how important the work group is to each busboy, but also how it functions to insulate members and to sanction them in extreme circumstances.

Why Work Hard? Dimensions of Willingness

Since most workers (and undocumented workers in particular) usually must do what is asked of them to keep their jobs, whether or not they are eager to do it should be beside the point. But for unskilled workers whose jobs are loosely defined, the "attitude" a worker conveys can be an important quality that either adds to or detracts from his value as an employee (see Waldinger and Lichter 2003). Mexican immigrants in the United States are primarily manual laborers (only 4 percent are in management or business),[8] and their desirability as low-wage employees is determined less by qualities like education, training, and experience and more by qualities like reliability, flexibility, and attitude. Displaying a "good attitude" can give undocumented workers an advantage in low-wage job competition, and low-wage employers consistently compare Mexican workers favorably to American workers in terms of their "willingness" and capacity for hard work.[9] As one employer put it, "'[I]mmigrant men are going to work much harder and take more crap than any black man...will take'" (Waldinger and Lichter 2003:177). The Lions are well aware that having a "good attitude"—often described as being willing to work or wanting to work hard—is an integral part of their job. Luis says that, "Wanting to work is very important because someone who doesn't want to work won't work hard. On the other hand, a person who works hard, who likes his work, that makes him work better, he wants to go to work. In fact, for me the best quality that a busboy can have is a desire to work." At restaurants like Il Vino, the Lions' "willingness" to work hard is encouraged both directly and indirectly by their unauthorized status.

Many workers, like Alejandro, Leonardo, and Omar, acknowledge and resent that undocumented status constrains their employment opportunities and forces them to be compliant and willing. Leonardo says, "When you come from Mexico and you don't have anything, all you have to offer is that you are a good worker and you want to better yourself." Omar agrees and says that, for undocumented workers, being pliant can make the difference between keeping or losing a job: "They know we are illegal, so if I complain, what do you think they will say to me? 'There's the door if you don't like it.'"

Yet these workers also believe that having a good work ethic can reduce or even overcome the vulnerability associated with being undocumented. Leonardo continues, "If you're a good worker, nothing, not even being illegal, will ever affect you." Luis concurs: "Not having papers doesn't affect you [at Il Vino]. If you work hard and you know what you're doing, the bosses themselves are going to say, 'Oh this guy works hard, let's promote him.'" Indeed, busboys at Il Vino receive significant material and social benefits for working hard. The busboys earn tips from waiters and waitresses, who are more likely to tip generously when they are pleased with their busboys' work performance. They also receive considerable esteem from their American coworkers and managers, extending the benefits of working hard beyond economy and into the realm of autonomy and respect. For example, Rene observes that: "[The bosses] are always noticing who works and who doesn't work. And when you win them over, they don't watch you anymore, they give you—you win their respect." As I explore in more depth in the next chapter, gaining esteem for being a hard worker can enhance the dignity of undocumented immigrants who are highly stigmatized as "illegal aliens," while gaining autonomy and respect on the job may be particularly important for undocumented workers who are subject to constant and arbitrary supervision.[10]

Cultivating a reputation as hard workers also helps undocumented workers monopolize employment opportunities in the low-wage job market. Alejandro has had nearly twenty years of experience working in restaurants and has been busboy, busboy manager, and—unique among his friends—a waiter during this time. Alejandro has learned one thing well: he can manipulate stereotypes of Mexican immigrants as hard workers to promote employment for himself and his friends. He described one situation in particular to me, in which the owners of Uncle Luigi's had opened a second restaurant and hired a young, all-white bus staff:

And [the managers] told me, "They cannot handle it, [and] there's twelve [of them]. I want you to go over there and teach them how to work good."...I went down to the office and I said, "If you want to keep all these people working, you're going to need them. I can do, I'll bring five, six of my friends and we can do all this work. So you decide. You want to keep twelve people and not get the job done, or six guys and get the work done, and probably be cheaper for you." [The owner said], "Done. Get them."

Alejandro wielded stereotypes of Mexican immigrants as particularly hard workers to persuade his boss to hire his friends. For Alejandro and his co-immigrant friends, a "willingness to work hard" is a special feature of their labor power that they can strategically draw on to make their labor more attractive to employers.

Consent and Contradiction

Working hard supplies both material and non-material benefits for the Lions, but it creates contradictions for them as well. For example, while the Lions perform a willingness to work, they are reluctant to see themselves as deferential. In fact, they develop narratives that emphasize Mexican workers' physical bravery and resistance to abusive treatment. When the Lions workers sit around together and have a beer after work, they relish telling "war stories" in which a Mexican worker heroically confronts an abusive boss. These narratives are usually David vs. Goliath-style stories in which a Mexican worker stands up to an abusive boss, who is usually left cowering in fear. Invariably, the worker also loses his job. Luis remembers a conflict that occurred when he was a dishwasher at Uncle Luigi's:

> We were really busy in those days and sometimes we would get behind on washing the pots and [the boss] would scream at us, "Move! Fucking wetbacks, move! Move, motherfuckers!" He was an asshole and no one liked him. Whenever he got angry he would come into the kitchen and take it out on the wetbacks. The other dishwasher who worked with me was bigger than me, taller and thicker. And one day he said to the boss, "You're not going to talk to me like that." He was tired of the insults, he was on the brink. And so they were about to fight but the managers called the police. The police came and the managers told them that the Mexican was fired but refused to leave. So they fired that guy; well, he quit really.

Lalo recounted a story in which he threw food in his abusive manager's face:

> Once, I was working at a Chinese restaurant and it was always really busy. So you had to be really quick preparing the pork, the

vegetables, the shrimp, everything. And the owners were really nice, if you worked hard they noticed it and were really nice to you. But there was a kitchen manager who was a slave-driver and I had problems with him. He got mad at me one day and we got into it, and well, I couldn't take it any more and I threw a basket of shrimp in his face. Ha ha. And they fired me. They fired me. Ha ha.

Even though the Lions rarely engage in physical violence, these "war stories" repudiate any notion that they are passive or meek. Like most war stories, these are probably exaggerated but are nevertheless significant in the context of vulnerability that undocumented status confers on these workers. Narratives about standing up to the boss, challenging him physically, and putting one's job at risk highlight workers' self-respect and reveal that their "willingness to work" has its limits.

These limits are particularly revealed when workers discuss their plans for the future: Alejandro, Rene, Chuy, Manuel, and Luis have all expressed a desire to get a union job. Tellingly, they state their goal as "getting a union job," as opposed to work as a union carpenter or brick-layer or electrician, indicating that they are at least as concerned about being part of a union collective as they are about the work itself. For Rene, the appeal of being in a union has as much to do with autonomy as job security. He explains that, "If I get a job with the union, then when somebody asks, 'Where do you work?' I can tell them, 'Oh, I'm Local 399,' instead of 'I work for this guy or that guy.' Then you don't belong to anybody, it's more of a professional job." Workers' goals of unionization suggest that, under different circumstances, these "willing workers" might not be so different from more politicized immigrants described elsewhere.[11]

Ultimately, cultivating a social identity as hard workers provides several short-term advantages for undocumented Mexican workers, including control over the composition and organization of their work group and a measure of financial stability and social esteem. Yet a reputation as hard workers also has unintended implications for undocumented workers. While being known as "hard workers" has the benefit of making the Lions indispensable at their jobs, it has the side effect of reproducing various exploitative aspects of their work, including intensification of their labor characterized by increasing workloads for the same pay.

Notes

1. De Genova 2005; Gamio 1971 [1930]; Gutierrez 1995; Heyman 2001.
2. Coutin and Chock 1997; De Genova and Ramos Zayas 2003; Waldinger and Lichter 2003.

3. De Genova 2005; Neckerman and Kirschenman 1991; Waldinger and Lichter 2003.

4. Gutierrez 1995; Moss and Tilly 2001; Waldinger and Lichter 2003.

5. See also di Leonardo 1998; Gershon and Taylor 2008 for critiques of this use of culture.

6. While anthropological notions of culture usually avoid this kind of naturalization of inequality and difference, Appadurai (2004:60) notes that culture in an anthropological sense has typically referred to "one or other kind of pastness"—beliefs and behaviors that are presumably traditional, slow to change, and permanently present in a local, bounded social group. This notion of culture has been criticized for assuming distinctions between groups of people—and homogeny within them—that are, at best, amorphous and fluid (Appadurai 1996, 2004; Douglas 2004; but see Rosenblatt 2004). Further, traditional anthropological conceptions of culture may diminish the role of Western domination and expansion in the creation, differentiation, and study of putatively bounded cultural groups (Gupta and Ferguson 1997). In response, anthropologists have increasingly turned their attention to the ways in which shared meanings and social identities are continuously created and recreated in everyday interactions (e.g., Gershon and Taylor 2008; Rao and Walton 2004; see also Willis 1977). A conception of culture as "those differences that either express, or set the groundwork for, the mobilization of group identities" (Appadurai 1996:13) emphasizes the situational, dynamic construction of norms, boundaries, meanings, and group identities and the way that these take shape as part of broader economic and sociopolitical landscapes (Rao and Walton 2004; Sen 2004). This is not an entirely new use of "culture," as it strongly resembles the "shop-floor culture" that Burawoy (1979) describes in his ethnography of factory workers.

7. See also Adler 2005; Fine 1996; Stepick and Grenier 1994.

8. Pew Hispanic Center 2009.

9. De Genova and Ramos-Zayas 2003; Hondagneu-Sotelo 1994, 2001; Portes and Rumbaut 1996:41.

10. Of course, being esteemed for being a hard worker and being stigmatized are not contradictory. Gutierrez (1995) shows how racial stereotypes about Mexican workers in the U.S. have historically been used to justify their placement in difficult and degraded jobs (see also Pedraza and Rumbaut 1996).

11. E.g., Brodkin 2007; Smith-Nonini 2007; Zlolniski 2003, 2006.

CHAPTER SIX

Los Número Uno
Identity, Dignity, and Esteem

THEY'RE GOOD PEOPLE: LALO

My name is Lalo. I'm from León, Guanajuato, Mexico. In Mexico, we don't have a lot of money, but we live well because we own our own house. That's a big help because you don't have to pay rent, just bills. And the money that I made was enough to support my kids and the house. With what my wife earned, we bought clothes and other necessities.

I have nephews here, and they were filling my son's head with thoughts of coming to Chicago. So my wife said, "Look, why don't you go for a while and we could save money to buy a little business, our own business?" I didn't want to come, but my son was like, "Yeah! Yeah!" We couldn't let him come by himself because he's so young, only fourteen, and it's very dangerous and he's immature. So I said okay, but immigration authorities [la migra] grabbed us on the Arizona border. We were going to go back home when some other guys contacted us and passed us through Mexicali.

In Mexico, I used to work as a welder in a tannery. A tannery is where they prepare leather to make shoes. And it's a hard job, but it pays well. The problem is that there are so many people who need jobs, and there's not enough work. So people say, "We're going to go to the U.S. because there's work there." When they come to the U.S., the first thing they do is get a job washing dishes in a kitchen. You put in your time, you move up the ladder, you could be a cook, or even higher. And it pays well. I have a friend who is from León who has been here like twelve years, and he's the chef at an important restaurant. And they pay him well. And so he said "I did what I came here to do; now I'm going back to Mexico." And that's how it is. So he leaves, but there will be another person under him who is waiting for his opportunity. And the white bosses see that.

There are white bosses that are very good. And there are Mexican bosses that are really good too. There are white bosses that are bad and Mexican bosses that are bad. The worst part about it is that it hurts you, because if you're Mexican, you're not begging for money, you're working for it.

The bosses that I have right now hold the busboys in very high regard, more than the white workers. They have a lot of confidence in them. For example, when Alberto came back from Mexico the last time, it gave me a lot of pleasure to see that Colleen saw him and was like, "Hi, welcome back! Here is your job!" She was happy to see him, and I felt good because he's such a good worker. But still and all, you have to win your boss over. What I say is that if I'm going to win over my boss, I will do it with work and not with gossip, not by telling them, "This guy doesn't do this right, that guy didn't do that."

One day the bosses might tell you, "Very good job," and so you say to yourself, "Okay, now I have won the bosses' trust." You always work the same way, you always do the same things. When there's no work, you don't do as much, of course, but you always do the same things. So when there's a lot of work and everything is good, they say, "Oh, great, cool, these guys are great workers." And so you think that the boss trusts you. But then whatever little thing that the managers or someone else tells them, even if it's about a very good worker, he'll get in trouble. For any little thing.

Do I consider myself a hard worker? Yes, I do. Maybe I'm not as good as the other busboys where I work, but I make an effort. For one thing, and I'm not trying to make excuses, but ever since I can remember, since I was seven years old, I have worked. So now I'm thirty six, and I'm tired. That's the truth. So if I seem a little slow, it's because I'm tired. But I do the best job I can. I'm not going to tell you that I'm as good as the other guys, because I know how they work and I respect them. Maybe if they came to work with me [as a welder in Mexico], then it would be the other way around. But I am learning to do the job that they are good at, so yes, I consider myself a good worker. And I like to work—well, I don't like it, because it wears me down; but it's my job, it's what I get paid for, and I do it with pleasure. Because if I go to work and I'm angry, like some people, "Oh, I have to wash the bathrooms and take out the garbage," it's worse for me. I like it. I like to learn new things so when I go back home I can open a small restaurant.

How would I describe the Lions? That's hard because each one has his own style, his own personality. But they have all helped me and been really cool with me. They have all supported me. Maybe it's because we're all from the same place. Maybe. But I've also seen them help other people who aren't from the same town. They are all good guys, good guys in the sense of good workers. They are workers, that's the word. They are really hard workers. If there's work, they tackle it, they beat it down. Always. They're workers and good people. I'm not sure why they help me so much. Maybe it's because they've struggled just like I have. Whether you're Catholic or not, like they say, help me and I will help you [*ayúdame que yo te ayudaré*]. If you help me today, tomorrow I will help you if I can. So that's how it is here: the guys that work with me are younger than me, and they've helped me so much, telling me how to do the job, sticking up for me with the boss. They were going to fire me once and the other guys said, "No, we need him." That was a big help for me.

The difference between Mexicans and white guys is that white guys don't want to work. They don't want a job that's too hard, or far away, or low paying. Here they blame everything on undocumented people. But that's why we get the jobs, because they know that we want to work no matter what it is. Yeah, there are white guys who are good workers too, and not all Mexicans are good. There's a bit of everything. But the American boss always prefers Mexican workers.

No matter what, people will still keep coming here: and no matter what, the bosses are still going to need them. I heard on the television that they say there are twelve million undocumented people here who don't pay taxes.[1] How much money are they losing? So the government says, we are losing so much money that we could use for hospitals, schools, for undocumented people themselves. Okay, so don't make them citizens, but at least give them permission to work. The country wins because they get their taxes, and the restaurants and factories can increase their production—everyone wins. The U.S. is a nation of immigrants. So if they build a wall, the Mexicans will build a tunnel. Or a higher ladder. They'll always be jumping the border.

The three previous chapters explored how the Lions navigate the terrain of work and society in the United States through their everyday activities. This chapter examines the more subjective side of workaday life—investigating how undocumented workers develop identity and dignity that engages and negotiates their political, racial, and class-based circumscription.

Race, Class, and Illegality: Structural Dimensions of Mexican Immigrant Identity

In the United States, the ascription of people into racial categories has been particularly acute in the creation of the categories "black" and "white," but when immigrants arrive in the United States, they are racially classified too. These classifications subsume immigrants' regional, class, ethnic, and national differences so that, for example, Latin American immigrants in the United States are typically racialized as "Latino," "Hispanic," or "Black," collapsing differences among their self-ascribed ethnic identities and places of birth.[2]

The construction of a "Mexican" identity in the United States is both emblematic of this process and historically unique. It is emblematic in that Mexican residents of the United States have undergone a racialization process that conflates nuances in their regional, ethnic, class-based, and gendered backgrounds.[3] For example, national distinctions between Mexicans and other Latin Americans are generally not recognized in U.S. government programs, census data, and official publications, and Latin Americans tend to be treated as a homogenous cultural group.[4] In fact, the very label "Hispanic" was created at the height of Chicano militancy in 1969 to submerge the particular histories of Mexicans, Puerto Ricans and other Spanish speakers into a broad and generic cultural group, weakening their particular political demands.[5] Many Mexican immigrants, Mexican Americans, and other Latin Americans in the United States have responded by forming just such a "Latino/a" community that generates solidarity and feelings of shared experience. Divisions within this community, however, have anything but disappeared; Latino/a identity is nuanced with respect to class, gender, nationality, and ethnic origin.

Homogenization of Latin Americans can have regional particularities; because of the large Mexican population in the Chicago area, Latin American workers in Chicago are often labeled "Mexican," even when they may actually be from Central or South American countries. The Lions and their co-workers and friends all call themselves "Mexicans" and rarely use the term "Latino/a." In this chapter, I also prefer to describe the Lions as Mexican rather than Latino for two reasons: first, to avoid conflating the experiences of Mexican immigrants with the experiences of all other Latin American immigrants, and second, because "Mexican" is associated with the working class and illegal status in a way that "Latino" is not, and these are two important components of the Lions' social identities.

The formation of a Mexican identity in the United States is historically unique because of the particular association of "Mexican" with working-class and illegal status.[6] The salience of illegal and working-class status to Mexican identity can be explained by the association of Mexicans with a long-term labor migration that is increasingly dominated by unauthorized entries. While other immigrant groups have also tended to be associated with the working class, the perpetuation of Mexican migration as a labor migration, combined with increasing restrictions on legal entry and enforcement-oriented "operations" concentrated on the southern border, has collapsed Mexican/illegal/working class identity in a historically contingent way.[7]

In recent years, highly publicized and polarizing debates about immigration have relegated popular perceptions of Mexican immigrants in the United States into two widespread one-dimensional types. Although one stereotype is putatively positive and the other very negative, all stereotypes reduce people to one-dimensional ideas about their difference and can perpetuate segregation and dehumanization.

The first widespread stereotype of Mexican immigrants in the United States can be called "Mexicans as illegal aliens." This conception of Mexican immigrants identifies them as iconic illegal immigrants and stigmatizes them as lawless, unclean, uneducated, and threatening interlopers who paradoxically steal jobs and leech public assistance.[8] As the fodder of conservative cable news shows, radio programs, and high-profile local political campaigns, this stereotype has wide popular currency. As a result, Latin American immigrants in the United States have become especially vulnerable to social alienation, exploitation, harassment, and hate crimes in recent decades.[9]

The second prevailing stereotype can be termed "Mexicans as hard-working immigrants." This conception of Mexican immigrants locates them in hegemonic narratives of "America as a nation of immigrants" and "America as a land of opportunity." Mexican immigrants, even the undocumented, are portrayed as sympathetic figures who have earned a moral claim to American citizenship by striving to improve their lives just as generations have done before them. This stereotype emphasizes Latin American immigrants' religiosity, family orientation, and work ethic and is frequently promoted in immigrant rights discourses.[10] Both of these stereotypes—"Mexicans as illegal aliens" and "Mexicans as hard-working immigrants"—continue to abound and are applied (sometimes simultaneously) to Mexican workers in restaurants like Uncle Luigi's and Il Vino.

Mojarones and Pacos: Race, Class, and Illegality at Il Vino

At Il Vino, categories of work are mapped onto categories of race, class, and legal status, segregating Mexican workers and reinforcing their circumscription on the job. This segregation is so persistent that the busboys at Il Vino are widely referred to as "the Pacos," a clear reference to their Mexican origins. Although the busboys have been complicit in reproducing racialized stereotypes of themselves as very hard workers (as described in the last chapter), it is ultimately the managers, not the workers, who decide who gets to work and in what jobs. Thus, in this section I explore managements' beliefs about their Mexican immigrant employees.

There are three levels, or "tiers," of management at Il Vino. The highest tier is "general manager"; the general manager oversees all other managers and is responsible for maintaining seamless operations between different sections of the restaurant. The second tier is occupied by two "floor managers" who are responsible for the minute-by-minute operation of the restaurant and who take care of customer requests and complaints. The third tier consists of "section managers," who are in charge of segments of restaurant operations. Among section managers, there is a "server manager," who supervises the hosts, servers, and bartenders; a "party manager," who takes care of catering, entertainment, and banquet parties; and a "kitchen manager," who is in charge of the kitchen staff and the menu. Notably, the kitchen staff mostly hails from Jalisco, Mexico, and is Spanish monolingual. The kitchen manager also speaks Spanish, but he is Puerto Rican, not Mexican. Since none of these managers is formally in charge of the busboy staff, busboys have some autonomy in how they manage their work group, but they are also subordinate to the entire management staff, as all managers interact with the busboys and give them instructions throughout the workday.

The management staff at Il Vino generally agrees that the Mexican busboys are "the best workers that we have." The general manager describes them as "phenomenal workers," while one floor manager says that the busboys are "awesome" and "the backbone of the place." Managers frequently explain the Mexican workers' superior work ethic in terms of their "culture," but they also acknowledge that Mexican workers have financial needs that "motivate" them to work hard. The kitchen manager explains, "You know what you're going to get from a Mexican immigrant, especially straight from Mexico; if they're coming from Mexico, they're in need.... So, out of necessity, they're going to give you a bigger effort than somebody here who's established." A floor manager agrees, "It's motivation. It's not confidence; anyone could do the job. It's just a matter of if you're willing to be a hard worker. If you're lazy, if you've had everything handed to you your whole life, [you won't be as motivated]. . . . If [the busboys] had papers, they might not be such hard workers." Whether they believe that work ethic is cultural or compelled by need (or both; there need be no contradiction here), the management staff agrees that the busboys are more self-motivated, hard working, and compliant than other workers at Il Vino. This raises an apparent paradox—why are the hardest workers at the restaurant also in the lowest-paid positions? Why aren't busboys rewarded for their hard work with pay raises and promotions?

Some of the managers attribute the Mexican workers' circumscription into the lowest paid jobs to an established association of Mexican immigrants with certain jobs. The general manager says that theoretically he would promote a Mexican busboy to server, but such an arrangement would violate the restaurant industry's "common sense." He explains, "I think that, and once again it's going to be stereotypical, but I think that people look at the industry and think that Hispanics are supposed to be busboys, which means in turn that they're going to be phenomenal at it." A floor manager agrees and says, "Just judging by experience, at least in my business, [the bosses] prefer the Mexican worker over any other race for the jobs that they do, because they know they're getting pretty much an honest day of work out of them compared to what they'd get from somebody else." Management also attributes workplace segregation to the Mexican workers themselves, who are presumed to want to work as busboys. The kitchen manager explains, "I would say it's a comfort thing, where if there's a group of Mexicans working in one area, it's really hard for them not to work with them. . . . If given a chance to choose, they're going to work where they're more comfortable, and I think that comfort is going to be where their people are at." In a twist on perceived preferences, the general manager attributes the Mexican workers' circumscription to the social pressure of their work group. He says, "I don't think they'd want to [wait tables]. The other guys would make fun of them or would laugh at them, for sure they would give them a hard time."

But managers have other reasons for keeping Mexican workers in back-of-the-house jobs. One frequently cited factor is a perceived language barrier, which would make it difficult for Mexican workers to interact frequently with English-speaking customers. When they are asked what holds back Rene and Roberto, who are highly fluent in English but still work as busboys, managers fall back on economic rationales for the segregation of Mexican employees. The kitchen manager explains that he wishes the economy in Mexico was better, but adds that "at the same time, if it weren't that bad, then how many businesses [in the U.S.] would go under because you can't afford, you really can't afford the wages of an American to do what a Mexican does. You would have to pay a pot scrubber fifteen dollars when you can pay [a Mexican] guy seven dollars to do the same job." Similarly, the catering manager argues that the restaurant needs Mexican workers because Americans like him disdain low-wage jobs: "It's sad to say, they're coming here to try to better themselves and they're doing jobs that other people would look down on. You know, I'm not going to mop a floor, I'm not going to clean a toilet, where this is just an individual looking to pay some bills and survive, and I don't think they look at jobs as being demeaning. They just look at it as a job, and it's better than what they had before." Even when the segregation of Mexican workers is glossed as workers' preferences, managers widely and openly acknowledge that there is an economic dimension to maintaining them in the worst-paid jobs.

The managers at Il Vino effectively rationalize exploitation of undocumented workers, as their beliefs about Mexican immigrants' preferences, talents, and economic needs map onto their perceptions of what a good busboy is, reinforcing and justifying the employment segregation of the immigrant staff. Segregation and homogenization of Mexican employees also perpetuate stereotypes of Mexican workers, as managers fit the busboys into their preconceptions of what Mexican workers should be like. The implications of racial stereotyping of the Mexican busboys become apparent when the usual order of things is shaken up. The story of "Frank" is worth telling at length, because it demonstrates how racialization works at Il Vino, and how work behaviors are interpreted in ways that reinforce management's assumptions.

To date, Frank has been Il Vino's only long-term "white" busboy, a young working-class man who was initially hired to clean during the day. Frank worked for many months alongside Rene, who was bussing lunch shifts, and the two men formed a friendship. Eventually, Frank asked for Rene's help to become a busboy. Rene spoke to the general manager and he reluctantly agreed, though he said that he doubted that Frank would be able to "keep up with the Pacos." But Frank did become a busboy, and he says that the all-Mexican bus staff "took me right in, I jumped in, I did what they asked me to do, and I worked hard, and they appreciate that a lot." Not only was being a busboy more "exciting," but Frank says that he felt a sense of belonging and pride as he earned his co-workers' esteem as a busboy: "Everybody was giving you praise, like, 'Oh, you guys bust your ass,' you know, 'I've never seen people work as hard as you guys.' And, you know, it felt good. It was like, you felt like you were appreciated." Even so,

Frank had to contend with stereotypes that, as a white man, he wouldn't be able to "keep up with the Pacos." He says, "For a white kid to come on and work just as hard as these Mexican guys, I mean it's kind of shocking. Because it's hard to keep up with those guys, you know, they don't stop. They're like zoom, zoom. You know, I'm happy though, I kind of showed them, I guess, and proved myself. There's self-respect there." Unlike other "white guys" who have worked briefly as busboys at Il Vino, Frank did well in the job and worked as a nighttime busboy for nearly three years.

One day, after some server complaints about the bus staff, management decided to appoint a formal busboy manager. This position would be different from the de facto head busboy that had characterized the informal leadership of the busboys' work group intermittently for several years. This position involved a formal appointment, with a pay raise and recognition as a manager, including participation in management meetings. The general manager offered Frank the job, even though Rene, Roberto, Alberto, Chuy, and Leonardo all had more seniority than he did. The racist dimension of promoting the only white busboy to manager was not lost on anyone, and to make matters worse, the same week that Frank's promotion was decided, Chuy was fired for getting into a fight with a kitchen worker, and Rene quit. Although Rene says that his reason for leaving was a higher-paying construction job, those closest to him, including his wife, Molly, and brother Chuy, suspect that Rene was hurt that he was suddenly made subordinate to his less-experienced friend. Angry at Chuy for fighting and Rene for leaving, the owners and the general manager then decided to systematically replace the Mexican busboys with "neighborhood kids," which is code for "white workers." Within two months, only Roberto and Leonardo remained of the original group; the rest of the busboys were young white workers.

The new arrangement was roundly considered a disaster. The bus service rapidly declined, as busboys with many years of experience were replaced by teenage workers who were new to the restaurant business. The general manager described the white busboy staff as "horrible" and "clueless," and servers and managers alike voiced their displeasure with the decision. Less than eight months after the decision to replace the Mexican workers with "neighborhood kids" was made, the general manager called Rene. Per Tony's wishes, he asked Rene to come back to Il Vino and even told him he could name his own terms. Rene negotiated for health insurance and a small raise in his hourly rate, and management agreed. The general manager then asked Chuy to come back too, and the re-replacement began. Within two weeks, the busboy staff was once again all-Mexican-immigrant, as Alberto returned from Mexico and the surviving white busboys were fired. Frank was removed as busboy manager and offered a daytime bartending position earning less in tips than he had as a night-time busboy. For his part, Frank never liked being manager and is nostal-gic for the days when he worked as a busboy "with the guys." The busboy staff continues today to be all-Mexican-immigrant, with the core group intact, and without a permanent, formal manager.

At Il Vino, busboy is a racialized job category, and the busboys are racialized workers. This is demonstrated in the strict racial segregation of Mexican workers in busboy and kitchen jobs, in the manager's comment about Frank working with "the Pacos," in management's decision to pro-mote the only white busboy to manager and replace the Mexican workers with white workers, and in the subsequent decision to replace the white workers with Mexican workers again. In this case, we see two different ste-reotypes of Mexican immigrants at play. The first, "Mexican men as imma-ture and temperamental," came to the fore after Chuy fought another worker and Rene quit, and it was used to justify the replacement of Mexican work-ers with white workers. The second stereotype, "Mexicans as really hard workers," won out when the white workers did not do well and was used to justify replacing white workers with Mexican immigrants. At Il Vino, the busboys' strengths and weaknesses—of Mexican and white workers alike—were more associated with their putative ethno-racial characteristics than with their experience, training, or motivation to do the job.

It is in this context of racialization and stigmatization that undocu-mented people like the Lions make sense of who they are and what they are doing. But, as Heyman (2001) points out, "identifications are not the same as identities" (135), and workers develop complex and contradictory perceptions of themselves as they face subordination, respond to stereo-typing, and construct social identities in the United States. The remainder of this chapter considers how the Lions cultivate dignity and self-esteem as they consider themselves in relation to other groups of workers in the context of broader narratives about illegal immigration and America as a land of opportunity. [11]

The Dignity of Hard Work

Working hard provides several immediate benefits for workers—it pro-motes their job security, augments their income, and makes their work-day go by faster—but it is also a critical source of workers' self-esteem and an integral component of their identities as working-class men. The Lions emphasize the integrity of hard work, and they argue that working hard is an honorable approach to upward mobility that requires bravery and stamina. As they call attention to the economic contributions that they make to U.S. society as low-wage workers, the Lions also address and rebut anti-immigrant arguments that undocumented workers drain the U.S. economy and take jobs from U.S. citizens.

In the following quote, Lalo expresses a widely held view that highlights his identity as a worker as it counters stereotypes of undocumented immigrants as criminal:

> Jumping the border—yes, it's a crime. But is it criminal? One thing is to kill, or steal something. Okay, I'm stealing something in the sense that I am on your land without permission, but I didn't come to kill, I didn't come to steal, I didn't come to hurt anyone. But they don't want to see it that way. So, yes, jumping the border, I know that I'm committing a crime, but it's not the same as if I work for you and you don't pay me. That is stealing. And we are human beings and we should help each other. And you should pay me because I'm doing work for you. But you take advantage and don't pay me because I'm undocumented, and I can't do anything about it. You just call immigration, or the police, and it's over. That's a robbery, anyway you want to look at it. That's stealing, that's a crime.

In this comment, Lalo not only reaffirms the image of the "hard-working Mexican," he makes a moral argument against the abuse of undocumented labor. As the threat of immigration enforcement is ever-present in the labor relations of undocumented workers, many workers like Lalo perceive such laws as tools in their exploitation. Alejandro remarks that "the bosses know you don't have papers, and they use it. That's why they pay you what they pay you, because you cannot ask for more money." In contrast to exploitative employers, the Lions emphasize that they have an ethical approach to getting ahead: good, old-fashioned hard work.

The Lions emphasize the respectability of hard work, and they draw very strong boundaries against suck-ups [*barberos*] and American workers, who they say will try to win the boss at any cost. The idea that undocumented Mexican workers have an ethical approach to self-improvement [*superándose*] at work is also emphasized in this quote from Lalo: "What I say is that if I want to win the boss, it's going to be with work, not by gossiping with him." The Lions' boundaries against "suck-ups" are so strong that workers who cause friction by gossiping or backstabbing are alienated from the social group. This happened to Rodolfo, a childhood friend of Rene and Chuy, who was effectively cut off from the resources of the group after being widely suspected of gossiping with the managers at Il Vino. Notably, his exclusion from the work group ultimately resulted in

Rodolfo's dismissal as an Il Vino busboy, as managers puzzled over why he was apparently unable to get along with the other workers. As the Lions express contempt for workers who backstab other workers to get ahead and emphasize their own ethical approach to work, they render hard work a moral activity that is worthy of dignity and respect.

The Lions also associate difficult labor with bravery and stamina and dismiss those whom disdain physical labor as "dirty." For example, while Lalo admits that he does not enjoy cleaning bathrooms, he also says, "It doesn't scare me. Because there are white guys who see vomit and say, 'No, no way.' Yes, it smells bad and it looks gross, but you're going to clean it, you're going to take a shower, [and] you're going to wash your hands. So it's not that dirty." As an undocumented immigrant, it may be far easier for Lalo to dismiss those who snub "dirty work" than to avoid that work himself. By equating willingness to work with integrity and bravery, these workers convert socially degraded work into a source of self-esteem.

The Lions frequently contrast their labor with that of American workers, who they typically conflate with "white" workers.[12] Because of the intense racial segregation of African Americans in the Chicago area, the Mexican workers at Il Vino rarely cross paths with African Americans and do not tend to see them as competitors in the labor market. Perhaps because they are largely based on inexperience, the Lions' attitudes toward African Americans run the gamut from reproducing disparaging stereotypes about African Americans' supposed unwillingness to work, to empathy with African Americans based on common experiences of racism in the United States, to bald curiosity. More than once, a Lion has asked me why poor African Americans do not want to work, believing that, since they (the Lions) have been able to obtain a job without papers, it must be easy for American citizens to get jobs if they want them. When African Americans do come up in conversation, they are usually the subject of some kind of observation—"Oh, there are a lot of blacks [*morenos* or *negros*] here today."—that is not overtly positive or negative.

The Lions are far more concerned with drawing boundaries against white workers [*gabachos*], whom they largely view as "lazy" and "privileged." They emphasize that Mexican workers, in contrast to whites, are more likely to be hard working and appreciative of opportunity. This comment from Alejandro highlights the distinction he perceives between Mexican workers' and white workers' approaches to work: "I think [white workers] score more points by doing other things than work, and we do the opposite, we do more work than other things, like sucking up to the boss." This racial distinction between Mexican and white workers is also illustrated in the following comment by Luis, in which he expresses a sentiment that is widely shared by the other Lions: "A Mexican works at a certain level, a certain rhythm, boom, boom, boom. And a white guy, no. A white guy is used to working slow, so when he gets tired of doing something, he stops and rests, you know? And then the wetbacks start to complain that he doesn't work well and stuff. It's what I'm telling you: an American is not worth as much as a Mexican."

The Lions believe that white workers are not held to the same standards of work that they are—that managers expect less from white workers and tolerate their laziness. In the following comment, Lalo reacts to Tony's complaint that he "looks tired:" "Yeah, I'm not saying that I'm not, because I am tired, but tell [Tony] to take a good look, okay, take a good look at the whites, how they walk around and they don't even do a good job.... How come he only says stuff to the wetbacks?" The Lions most frequently expressed the opinion that white workers are not hard workers when they compared themselves with white busboys who, they felt, were not contributing their share. Only Frank has been able to dispel the Lions' stereotypes about lazy white busboys and win long-term respect and camaraderie as a fellow busboy.

While the busboys reproduce racialized stereotypes of their labor, they are also aware that those stereotypes can justify unfair treatment, inequality, and exploitation. They acknowledge that there is nothing primordial about being a hard worker, and they frequently point out that race is not a good determinant of a person's work ethic. Roberto explains that for him, a person's capacity for work, not their race, is what makes them a good or bad co-worker: "There is no difference, none at all. If someone doesn't want to work, if they are black, or Latino, or African, or American, or Asian, if they don't want to work hard, they're not going to last. It doesn't matter what kind of person they are, what matters is if they work hard [si le echan ganas]." In interviews, the Lions often followed up stereotypical comments about Mexican workers' superior work ethic with a comment on variation among groups of workers. The following remark by Rene illustrates his ambivalence about race as a good indicator of work ethic: "Probably if you're waiting on help from a fellow Hispanic, somebody that you already know, he probably won't help you like you need;... the white guy [el gabacho], if you talk to him right, he will help you a lot." The Lions also say that not all undocumented Mexican workers are hard workers and readily recognize that many white workers do indeed work very hard.

In spite of their status as undocumented immigrants, the Lions have gained a high degree of social esteem from their co-workers at Il Vino. As I mentioned in the first chapter, the busboys regularly interact socially with their nonimmigrant co-workers, and several are involved romantically with white female co-workers. As this comment from the server manager illustrates, there are social norms at Il Vino that encourage respectful treatment of the busboys: "These [busboys] have been here for a long, long time, and if you come to a place and you see people treating them good, you're going to too, or you're an idiot. For one, because you don't want to be that asshole looking down on people who basically opened this place up and had a massive part in how successful it is." While the primary source of this esteem is the notion that the busboys are "the best workers," the Lions are also known as friendly, funny, and considerate young men.

In fact, the busboys' reputation as valuable workers who are worthy of respect is so strong that many of the servers are concerned about making a good impression on them! When I once casually mentioned to a new waitress that I had heard good things about her from the busboys, she expressed relief, saying how important it was to her that the busboys like her. On another occasion, a waitress who was displeased with Rene, who was her busboy that night, said that she would never complain about him to management since, "Rene is untouchable." The busboys are considered an integral part of the restaurant staff, and when Il Vino customers do or say things that may be considered disrespectful to the busboys, other employees are likely to defend them. Once, a couple of rather drunk customers had knocked their bread crumbs onto the floor and then laughed when Alberto came to sweep them up. Their waitress angrily told the customers to stop, saying, "You don't make extra work for our guys like that!" On another occasion, a customer accused Chuy of stealing or clearing (it wasn't clear which) his pack of cigarettes off of the table. The waiter defended Chuy, explaining to the customer that Chuy had worked there for a long time, was completely trustworthy, and certainly knew better than to throw away a full pack of cigarettes.

For their part, the busboys mostly like their white co-workers, particularly the service staff, and they socialize with them frequently. At closing time, it is quite common for the servers and busboys to sit around and have a drink (or several) together. Although the busboys tend to sit at one table and the servers at another, there is quite a bit of social interaction between the two groups. Busboys are regularly invited to social outings, including birthday parties and baseball games.

The busboys' relationship with the management staff is more ambivalent. While managers at Il Vino celebrate the busboys' "work ethic," they also express paternalistic and racist attitudes toward the busboys, calling them on occasion "my little guys" or "the Pacos." Leonardo says that he thinks the bosses at Il Vino see him as "just another poor wetback working for us." The busboys also resent what they see as some managers' reluctance to do actual work and their propensity to call the busboys for every little thing. In fact, some of the busboys have said that the worst thing about working at Il Vino is the constant haranguing by management staff on the walkie-talkie radios.

On the Margins of the "American Dream"

Valorizing hard work is not only an immediate panacea to compensate for doing degraded jobs, it is an integral part of the Lions' broader worldviews. Perhaps the most unexpected aspect of the Lions' lives is the degree to which they are integrated economically and socially into the broader U.S. society as workers. Unlike many inner-city young men in the United States (those featured in Philippe Bourgois' "In Search of Respect" [1996/2003] and Jay MacLeod's "Ain't No Makin' It" [1995] come to mind), the racialization of undocumented Mexican workers has not excluded them from the job market—in fact, the stereotyping of Mexican immigrants as superior low-wage workers has resulted in their *preferential* hiring in many low-wage industries. This immersion in an active working-class culture makes it possible for workers like the Lions to identify with larger working-class values and to aspire to middle-class status. In this context, developing a social identity as hard workers is not only in harmony with the Lions' value systems, it is consistent with their active participation in the U.S. labor force.

The Lions believe that winning over the boss by working hard has provided them with a degree of financial security, as well as respect, in spite of their status as illegal immigrants. This conceptual connection allows them to take personal credit for their good fortunes and feel like they have some control over their economic outcomes. Consequently, they gear their workplace strategies toward winning the boss [*ganándose al patron*] by doing extra work and always appearing "willing to work hard." The belief that hard work brings reward is affirmed by the structure of income distribution in restaurants like Il Vino. Busboys receive immediate, material feedback on their work in the form of tips, which draws a direct connection between effort and talent, on the one hand, and income, on the other. The busboys at Il Vino are also relatively highly paid, further enhancing a sense of personal reward and repressing a sense of collective subordination. The Lions' beliefs about work must also be considered in the context of their exclusion from workers' unions and compensation programs like unemployment benefits. The Lions and other undocumented workers live without the parachutes that provide citizen workers with a modicum of protection against unemployment and poverty. Perhaps, then, it is not surprising that they have learned to rely only on themselves and their most trusted friends for their economic well-being.

Not all the Lions express the same stance on work and power relations. In particular, Luis and Chuy are likely to snub behaviors that they feel are subservient, and they are sensitive to perceived exploitation and discrimination. This renders them more susceptible to charges that they have a "bad attitude" and has helped put both of these young men on the chopping block at Il Vino. Chuy, for example, is not good at always appearing eager to work and often fails to show the appropriate amount of enthusiasm for cleaning or doing extra tasks. This has led to rather amorphous server complaints about Chuy's "attitude" and to political arguments between Chuy and his more conservative brother, Rene. For his part, Luis asserts his dignity by refusing to "kiss the owner's ass" and "run around like an idiot." Even so, Chuy and Luis also agree that winning over the boss is important. Luis explains that he tries to win the boss so that… "if the boss knows that you work hard and he sees someone else who doesn't do it as well, then if there's a layoff one day and they're going to fire people, who do you think they're going to fire? The guy who works less. That's why, you could say, you win the boss." This is an unfortunately ironic comment from Luis, who was demoted and then later fired from Il Vino for failing to demonstrate an appropriate commitment to working hard.

In discussions about unauthorized immigration, the Lions articulate the argument that they are compelled to migrate because of circumstances beyond their control, but the ways in which they deal with those circumstances—by working hard, by being responsible, and by paying taxes, for example—are morally commendable. When I asked Roberto if he thought undocumented immigrants were criminals, he laughed, "If that's what they consider criminal, then we are criminals. But we come to work honorably, to live in peace. We don't bother anybody. I have never committed a crime in the U.S., and you have to behave yourself if you want to be a good citizen, as much here as in China or anywhere else. You have to be a good person." The Lions stress that they do not succumb to vices [*vicios*], such as spending money on luxuries and neglecting their families, or doing drugs, or cheating on their partners. They also emphasize the contributions that, as taxpayers, they make to the U.S. economy. Leonardo jokes that Mexicans have had a positive impact on the United States because "all the Mexicans are illegal [and] so they can't get their tax refunds, and all that money stays with the government. That's a lot of money from the Mexicans; they're probably using all that money to build that wall [on the border]."[13] By highlighting their moral fortitude and economic contributions to U.S. society, the Lions address and rebut the arguments, made popular by anti-immigrant groups, that undocumented immigrants are threatening criminals or potential terrorists. By fulfilling American ideals and adopting American values, undocumented immigrants like the Lions make a normative appeal for citizenship rights.

More broadly, the Lions emphasize narratives of "America as a nation of immigrants" and "America as a land of opportunity" as they make sense of the opportunities they encounter and stake a claim for legitimacy as workers in the United States. Leonardo says, "I don't care if I'm illegal or whatever. Why not? Because this country gives you opportunities. If you take advantage of them, good for you, and if you don't, you're stupid. So I feel good that I have been able to take advantage of opportunities here." Ironically, the Lions' very exclusion from the polity as undocumented immigrants supports their belief in merit-based achievement, since the limitations they encounter are explained by their illegal status. That is, to the extent that these workers experience exclusion from opportunities in America, they believe that they are excluded because they are not actually American. Moreover, since they have been able to secure employment as undocumented workers, the Lions believe that anyone should be able to do it. For example, Lalo claims, "If I had papers, I would never be without work. But how many white guys do you see begging on the street corner who are strong, capable of working in a kitchen? Why don't they work? They're lazy." The illegalization of undocumented workers provides an easy justification for constraints on their opportunities that is *consistent* with the ideals of the American Dream. In spite of their resentment toward the ways in which undocumented status constrains their opportunities, these workers widely affirm a belief in "America as a land of opportunity," and they generally believe that they will be able to attain middle-class status if they can adjust their legal papers. As the prospect of comprehensive immigration reform draws near, the Lions are cautiously optimistic about their futures as U.S. workers.

Gendered Identity and the Honor of Family Men

The Lions' social identities as hard workers and good citizens are deeply intertwined with their social identities as family men. The idea that family is the most important thing in life is a recurring theme in the Lions' discourse. They stress their commitment to family, the importance of family in their lives, and their sense of familial responsibility over all other considerations. The Lions are, by all accounts, mostly faithful to their partners and tend to define their masculinity by a sense of familial responsibility satisfied by financial provisioning.

Although the Lions lament long periods of time in which they were lonely for the company of women—usually just after arriving in the United States—all of the Lions are currently involved in serious relationships, except for Luis (who is involved in several nonserious relationships). As I mentioned earlier, six of the Lions—Alejandro, Chuy, Leonardo, Omar, Rene, and Roberto—are in serious romantic relationships with "white" American women. While there is no reason to doubt the sincerity of the emotional attachment between the Lions and their American partners, external factors may have also contributed to their pairing. First and foremost, there is a dearth of single Mexican women in the restaurant business; undocumented Mexican women who do come to the United States are often "hidden," working as nannies or maids in the private sector.[14] It is hard for the Lions, who work well over forty hours per week, to meet single female cohorts. Simply put, there may just be more white women available than Mexican women. Second, being with a white woman may offer status and financial security, since one enduring legacy of the Spanish conquest of Mexico is an association of lighter skin with wealth and power. Furthermore, the Lions' white girlfriends are all studying to be professionals whose incomes will make significant contributions to the Lions' middle-class aspirations. However, the Lions do not become involved with American women to "get papers." While the mistaken belief that marriage to an American citizen provides an easy path to legal status persists in wider society, the Lions are aware that this is no longer true. Under current immigration law, none of the Lions is eligible to "fix" his legal status within the United States, even with a citizen wife and children.

The Lions' fathering practices also provide a window into their beliefs about masculine gender roles. My ability to observe Lions with their children was limited by the geographical separation of father and children in the cases of Alberto, Luis, and Lalo and by the fact that Chuy, Leonardo, and Roberto do not have children yet. Any conclusions that I draw here are based only on observations of how the Lions interact with the children of Rene, Alejandro (who has partial custody of his son), and Manuel. Unlike the typical stereotype of the Mexican macho (see Gutmann 2007), Rene, Alejandro, and Manuel are active fathers who hold their infants, play with their toddlers, and "hang out" with their older children. For example, it is widely commented among the Lions that Rene and his two-year-old son Jacob Jose (J.J.) are attached at the hip [*siempre están pegados*] and that J.J. emulates his father in everything. Both Manuel and Alejandro are active fathers to their sons, and all of the Lions play with these children, who frequently accompany their fathers to social events and soccer games. (See Figure 6.1.) While I was in León, I noticed that Mexican men there interact

FIGURE 6.1 Wednesday soccer in the park: the backpacks make convenient goal posts, and Manuel's young sons are enthusiastic goalies. (*Courtesy of the author*)

a great deal with their children; it was not uncommon to see fathers carrying their infants and toddlers, or holding their older children's hands, as they strolled down the streets.

Fathering practices also reveal the limits of the Lions' gender progressiveness. In particular, there are apparent differences with the level of engagement that the Lions have with male and female children. They play with girls less, particularly as the girls get older, and they do not invite girls to accompany them as much on outings. There also appears to be a gendered division of labor concerning infant care: Molly says that Rene has never changed a diaper in his life.

Of course, the physical separation of Alberto, Lalo, and Luis from their children necessarily means that the responsibility of caring for children falls on mothers in Mexico. This can be a source of marital conflict, as wives feel resentful at this physical abandonment and overwhelmed at having to manage their households alone for extended periods of time. Interestingly, many of the wives of immigrant men that I met in Mexico have created informal but robust female communities that provide emotional support and child-caring help. For example, Alberto's wife lives with her mother, her sister (whose husband works in the United States), and her sister-in-law (whose husband also migrates back and forth between Mexico and the U.S.) in a single household in León. These women share household responsibilities and raise their children together. For their part, the men are emotionally conflicted about their familial responsibilities: they feel guilty, on the one hand, for being apart from their families and obligated on the other hand, to make dollars to secure their families' wellbeing (see also Pribilsky 2007).

This conflict is most apparent in Alberto. This is Alberto's third time in the United States—his last, he says. He and his wife reluctantly decided that he would return to Chicago to work when she became pregnant with their third child. He has yet to see his newest daughter, who will be nearly two years old by the time he expects to return to Mexico. He talks about his wife and daughters with great emotion—almost with awe. He says his wife is his best friend, the person that he admires and respects most in the world. Nevertheless, prolonged periods of separation are not easy on his marriage. Alberto feels torn between the need he always feels to stay a little longer and the need to be physically present in the life of his family. Alberto says he is trying to save up enough money so that when he returns to Mexico, he can open up a store of his own and be financially independent. But his savings are meager, and this goal has so far remained out of his reach.[15]

As undocumented Mexican workers in the United States, the Lions do not arrive freely able to position themselves as they choose in relation to the U.S. social structure. Instead, they contend with profound stereotypes, as well as racial, legal, economic, and social circumscription, and they negotiate their identity and self-worth within these subjective constraints. The Lions are not immune from either the stigma of being "illegal aliens" or the stigma of doing "dirty work." In fact, they develop multiple and various strategies for protecting themselves psychologically and defending their dignity and self-esteem.

The Lions utilize the racial and legal circumscription of their labor to help promote a reputation for themselves as hard workers. This strategy is fraught with contradiction: the Lions simultaneously reject the idea that race is a good indicator of work ethic and agree that Mexican workers are superior workers. While promoting racial stereotypes of themselves as hard workers may provide some short-term advantages, in the long run racial categorization constrains the Lions' life chances and reproduces the social inequalities that subordinate their labor.

The Lions' social and political circumscription from wider society also increases their reliance on one another for both material and emotional resources. In response, the Lions have created a social community with norms of mutuality and helpfulness; within these communities, they buffer themselves from disdain and promote values that uphold their sense of self-worth. In particular, work and relationships provide social space in which the Lions emphasize some normative beliefs—such as "hard work is a virtue" and "real men take care of their families"—and reinterpret others. This selective process allows the Lions to attain a sense of dignity in spite of being some of the most marginalized and vilified members of U.S. society. In fact, as I struggled with a title for this chapter, it was Chuy who suggested that it be called "*Los Número Uno*," or "The Number Ones."

Notes

1. Lalo is repeating a common misconception that undocumented workers don't pay taxes. In fact, between 70 and 80 percent of undocumented workers are estimated to pay taxes on their wages (Lalo is one of them), and all undocumented people pay sales and excise taxes (see Chapter 7).
2. Omi and Winant 1994; Portes and Rumbaut 1996.
3. De Genova 2005; De Genova and Ramos-Zayas 2003.
4. Portes and Rumbaut 1996:136; Romero 2002.
5. De Genova and Ramos-Zayas 2003.
6. De Genova 2005; De Genova and Ramos-Zayas 2003.
7. De Genova 2005; Ngai 2004.
8. Coutin and Chock 1997; De Genova 2005; Massey et al. 2002; Suarez-Orozco and Suarez-Orozco 1995; Vila 2000.
9. Pew Hispanic Center 2007; Suarez-Orozco and Suarez-Orozco 1995; Urbina 2009.
10. Coutin and Chock 1997. The work ethic of Latin American immigrants is often celebrated in contrast to African American workers, reinforcing racist stereotypes and economic marginalization of both, but to the particular detriment of the latter (see Waldinger and Lichter 2003; Steinberg 2005).
11. The concept of hegemony, first developed by Antonio Gramsci, has been particularly productive in studies of migration and transnationalism in linking the sociopolitical order with individual and group subjectivities. Hegemony refers to a system of ideas and practices, pervasive in all aspects of life, which reproduce the social order by making it seem natural and inevitable (Gramsci 1994). Living in a hegemonic society means that subjective constructions of identity are never free from the social positions of actors but are embedded in relations of power and position (see also Appadurai 1996; Basch et al. 1994; De Genova 2005; De Genova and Ramos-Zayas 2003; Portes and Walton 1981). Individuals and

groups struggle to enhance their positions in relation to the dominant sociopolitical order by defining themselves in certain ways and drawing boundaries against others. Group identity and solidarity tend to be particularly significant among people who are discriminated against by mainstream society.

Hegemonic concepts of race, ethnicity, nationality, class, and citizenship are reproduced, changed, and challenged as people construct identities and attempt to explain their status. When low-status groups draw boundaries against those "below" them, for example, they tend to repeat racial and status-based stereotypes and thereby subjectively reproduce hegemonic explanations for social inequality (what P. Gomberg, 2007, calls "the rationalization principle"). When comparing themselves to "those above," workers are more likely to reject or reinterpret mainstream explanations of inequality that justify their low status ("the ego-defense principle"). Instead, norms, values, and moral codes tend to emerge within low-status groups that provide alternative explanations for social inequality and may also supply sources of self-esteem (P. Gomberg 2007; Lamont 2000; MacLeod 1995 [1987]). For example, by promoting themselves as hard-workers and disparaging other groups who may be in competition with them for low-wage work as "lazy," the Lions can enhance their competitiveness in the labor market and boost their self-esteem. As they do so, they reproduce hegemonic concepts of individual meritocracy and the value of hard work.

12. See also De Genova 2005:8.
13. Leonardo is joking, but Chacon and Davis (2006) report that in early 2006, "the Arizona House Appropriations Committee approved a resolution that would attach an 8 percent state tax on electronic money transfers to Mexico. The tax, which will generate $80 million every year, will be used to pay for a double and triple-walled border fence between Arizona and Mexico" (164).
14. See Chang 2000; Hondagneu-Sotelo 2001; Romero 2002.
15. See the Epilogue.

CHAPTER SEVEN

Illegals and Criminals

Racism, Nativism, and the Criminalization of Low-Wage Labor

WE WETBACKS ARE PEOPLE WHO LIKE TO WORK: LEONARDO

I have six brothers and two sisters, and I am the youngest of all of them. I was the first one in my family to come here and, yeah, my family thought it was a good idea. The only one who had a problem with it was my mom. She was sad because I was the first one to leave and I was the baby in the family.

What I admire most about myself is that I can put up with a lot, and I just keep pushing forward. Why do I put up with it? Because I want to make a future for myself. I don't want to live like my parents or my brothers who get married and don't even have a house to take their wives to. I came here when I was nineteen, and that's the age when you spend your money on whatever you want. And I did that, but just for a little while, and then I started to think, why am I spending my money on stupid things? I should save it instead, save it to buy the things that I need. And now I can buy my house. So that's what I admire about myself, that I was never one of those kids who come here to just screw around.

We wetbacks are people who like to work and like to improve ourselves. When you come from Mexico and you don't have anything, all you have to offer is that you are a good worker and you want to better yourself. And when a Mexican comes here illegally and there are good opportunities, he will take advantage of them and improve himself. If you're a good worker, nothing—not even being illegal—will ever affect you. If you're a good worker and you take responsibility for what you're doing, the bosses themselves will appreciate you.

Since we're the ones who've been at Il Vino the longest, they give us preference, and they won't cut our hours or anything. But then they cut the newer guys' hours, and they don't realize that we need them. And so it fucks us, too, because we have to do more work. We end up doing double the work because the bosses don't want to hire anyone. And they don't give you benefits or anything.

Ruda, let me tell you what happened to me last night. Me and Gus were eating at this Mexican restaurant, and four white guys were there, and they start saying stuff to us: "Fucking wetbacks, fucking Mexicans," stuff like that. So we didn't say anything to them; but when we left, they followed us outside and they were calling us fucking Mexicans. And so I told them to go fuck themselves. They got mad and jumped us, two guys on Gus and two guys on me, and we started fighting them. The workers from the restaurant came and broke it up, but somebody called the police. So when the police got there, they didn't know anything about what had happened, and they started to arrest me and Gus; the white guys had left. And the cop is telling me, "You have a knife, you have a knife in your truck." But I didn't have anything. So the cop pulls out a gun on me and tells me and Gus to get out of the truck. We got out of the truck, and they grabbed me and threw me on the ground, they ripped my shirt and handcuffed me. Then they started asking the guys from the restaurant what had happened. They told them, "No, these guys didn't do anything, it was the white guys." Finally, the cops let us go, but they took the keys to my truck. And I told them, "Hey, give me my keys," and they were like, "No, we don't have your keys." So I looked for my keys for an hour before the cops came back and gave me back my keys. The cop was like, "Oh it was in my pocket; I didn't know I had it." What an asshole, you know? I don't know if that's racism or whatever, but they know we're wetbacks and we can't do anything about it.

Before I came here, I worked in an auto shop, fixing cars, painting cars. I liked it, but I think when I go back to Mexico, I will probably work in a factory. In a factory, they give you insurance and home loans and everything. But I want to make my life in Mexico.

In Chapter 2, I presented a history that shows how a combination of global economic practices and national border policies generates and sustains undocumented migration, which reproduces a reserve of especially vulnerable low-wage labor in developed regions. Chapter 2, then, was mainly concerned with describing the relationship of undocumented workers to the political economy of the nation-state, both in the United States and in Mexico. Chapters 3 through 6 focused on the daily activities of the Lions, a group of undocumented people who live and work in the United States. But what are the connections between undocumented immigrants like the Lions and the rest of us? Most U.S. citizens are not governmental policy makers or employers of immigrants but rather regular workers who are also struggling to make our lives as good as possible. How does the presence of so many undocumented workers affect people like us?

Myths and Realities

Misconceptions about undocumented immigrants abound. This is partly due to the complex and secretive nature of undocumented migration, which makes gathering reliable data a serious challenge. Furthermore, since undocumented immigrants tend to fly under the radar and are excluded from political power, assertions about them can be spread with little refutation. This creates an "anything goes" atmosphere, in which claims based on little, incomplete, or contradictory data are fueled by politicians and media personalities who boost their careers by railing against undocumented immigration.[1] There are two pervasive beliefs about undocumented immigrants—that they are bad for the U.S. economy and that they take jobs from citizens—which I examine in this first section.

Many Americans believe that undocumented immigration is bad for the U.S. economy. This belief is promoted by widespread claims that illegal immigrants cost American taxpayers billions of dollars each year in educational and medical expenditures. In point of fact, undocumented people do get sick sometimes, and since they disproportionately work in unsafe conditions, they are more likely than other workers to be injured on the job. Frequently lacking health insurance, undocumented people are less likely than legal residents and citizens to seek medical care when they need it, and they are often denied workman's compensation benefits by employers unwilling to bear the cost of their treatment. In some cases, the result is that seriously ill undocumented people are treated at hospital emergency rooms—at a cost to the U.S. taxpayer. Many undocumented people also have children and, like most parents, want their children to attend school. Thus, undocumented people do add children to the rolls of public schools, and the cost of public education increases accordingly.

According to restrictionist arguments, this creates a burden on U.S. taxpayers, who fund public education and emergency medical treatment through their tax dollars. But these arguments leave out a crucial piece of information: undocumented people are U.S. taxpayers too. In fact, undocumented people annually contribute billions of dollars in sales, excise, property, and income taxes to federal, state, and local coffers. The Social Security Administration alone receives subsidies in the amount of about seven billion dollars per year from undocumented immigrants—or about 10 percent of its annual surplus. Although approximately 20 to 25 percent of undocumented immigrants work "under the table" for cash only (as do some American citizens), most pay the same amount in income taxes as any other U.S. worker, and all pay sales, excise, and property taxes.[2]

Furthermore, while undocumented people pay into public programs with their tax dollars, they are barred from using almost all government services, including Social Security, Medicare, unemployment, federal housing programs, food stamps, Supplemental Security Income, Temporary Assistance for Needy Families, most Medicaid services, and the Earned Income Tax Credit. In fact, the only public services that undocumented people are eligible to use are emergency medical care under the Medicaid system, and elementary and secondary public education. Tax restructuring in the neoliberal era has meant that the cost of both emergency medical care and public education has been supported locally (not nationally) with reduced tax reserves, leaving these resources strained in small communities with growing populations—whether immigrant or native-born. But this strain is due to a mismatch between federal and local tax revenues and expenditures, accelerated during the 1980s, and not to immigration per se.

Undocumented immigrants contribute to the U.S. economy in many other ways as well. They work at very high rates, but on average their labor is poorly paid, keeping down costs of goods and services. And while many undocumented immigrants send large portions of their earnings to family members in their countries of origin, they also spend money in the United States. In fact, a 2006 *Time* magazine article reported that about 80 percent of undocumented immigrants' income is reinvested in the U.S. economy.[3] Furthermore, the consumption practices of undocumented immigrants in turn create jobs and revenues that further offset the impact of remittance outflows.

In sum, the evidence that undocumented immigrants make an overall net contribution to the U.S. economy is compelling, yet some researchers have published reports that make claims to the contrary.

One influential report published by the Center for Immigration Studies, a high-profile think tank that is also a vocal proponent for restrictionist legislation, argues that the low incomes of undocumented immigrants translate into low tax revenues and that when the costs of government services used by undocumented people and their families are deducted from these low tax revenues, the result is a net fiscal deficit. Interestingly, this report finds that the net contributions made by undocumented people to Social Security and Medicare are "unambiguously positive," and that low income, not illegal status, is responsible for creating the putative deficit.[4]

Even so, the study has a serious methodological flaw: it calculates the costs of undocumented immigration using a household model, which explicitly includes government services used by citizen family members and citizen children of undocumented people—and, according to Passel and Cohn (2009), about 73 percent of the children of undocumented immigrants are U.S. citizens. In fact, the study finds that "many of the costs associated with illegals are due to their American-born children, who are awarded U.S. citizenship at birth." That is, the "deficit" results from the use of services by American citizens who are the children of undocumented working-poor parents—a function of low income, not illegal status, and a problem for working-poor citizens as well. Moreover, the study's conflation of "illegals" with citizens (even if they are family members) is a serious sleight of hand—it should go without saying that U.S. citizens, by definition, are not illegal immigrants.

In spite of misleading reports by the CIS, most experts agree that undocumented immigration is a lucrative dimension of the U.S. economy. In fact, in a national survey of leading economists, 85 percent agreed that undocumented immigrants have a positive (74 percent) or neutral (11 percent) impact on the U.S. economy,[5] and a 2006 *Wall Street Journal* poll found that forty-four out of forty-six economists believe that illegal immigration is beneficial to the U.S. economy.[6] Pervasive and popular assertions that undocumented immigrants drain U.S. economic resources are at best poorly informed and, at worst, willfully misleading.

A related and more complex claim is that undocumented immigrants take jobs from U.S. citizens. One popular response to this argument is to assert that undocumented immigrants only take the jobs that American workers disdain. A summer 2006 poll by *Time* magazine showed that a majority of Americans believe that undocumented immigrant workers have jobs that U.S. citizens do not want.[7] This argument even has a correlate in anthropological scholarship that attributes large-scale labor immigration to native labor shortages, implying that if native workers were available and "willing" to do these jobs, the demand for immigrant labor would go away.[8] But the argument that undocumented immigrants take only the jobs that U.S. citizens are unwilling to do has two fundamental flaws. One, it is misleading. While undocumented immigrants do tend to occupy the bottom of the labor market, there is still job competition between immigrant workers and the native-born. Like undocumented immigrants, U.S. citizens are often "willing" to do low-wage, low-status, unpleasant, or dangerous work (fast-food restaurants, coal mines, and poultry processing plants come to mind; see Jefferson 2010). Moreover, a tighter labor supply brought about by restricting immigration would likely raise wages in lower-paying sectors and make them more attractive to citizens. The second flaw of this argument is its implication that undocumented labor is tolerable because it is exploitable. This may be a pragmatic response to anti-immigrant sentiment, but it undermines immigrant workers' claims to living wages and reinforces their exploitation. Ultimately, the argument that undocumented immigrants do only the jobs that no one else wants—which is popular in the immigrant rights movement—glosses over real hardships that citizen workers face on the job market and reinforces categorical subordination of undocumented labor. Does this mean that immigration should be restricted in order to improve the job prospects of citizens and ameliorate the exploitation of immigrants?

Many say yes. Some anti-racist scholars have argued that low-wage job competition, exacerbated by persistent large-scale immigration, is particularly harmful for African American workers who have historically faced exclusion in the U.S. job market. Stephen Steinberg (1995, 2005), for example, shows that economic expansion, first in industry and currently in service sectors, has not resulted in the full integration of black workers in the labor market, because immigration has supplied an abundant reserve of labor that allows employers to avoid hiring African American workers. In fact, the exclusion of black workers from the labor market is frequently justified by racist stereotypes that compare black workers unfavorably to immigrant workers.[9] Steinberg and others argue that justice for African Americans, in the form of full economic integration in the labor force, will only be realized by restricting immigration and tightening the labor supply—in effect forcing employers to hire African American workers.

This argument appears to have both practical appeal and ethical integrity: justice for black workers can be attained by restricting immigrant labor supplies. Leaving aside the humanitarian dimension of this argument for a moment, let us examine the practical claim: that restrictions on immigration will result in job opportunities for African American workers. The pragmatism of this measure must be important, since it is the main reason Steinberg favors it over the "unrealistic" push to unite the working class on a multiracial, international front (though he criticizes ideological compromise for political expediency elsewhere). But is it realistic to believe that policy makers will restrict immigration and improve the prospects of African Americans? To examine this question, let us turn briefly to an analysis of African American labor patterns in relation to immigration, and vice versa, since the civil rights movement of the 1960s.

The civil rights movement and the changes it engendered were supposed to end racial segregation and discrimination against African Americans and other minorities. By the mid-1960s, landmark civil rights legislation was being passed at the federal level: the 1964 Civil Rights Act ended legal segregation in public places and prevented employment discrimination, while the 1965 Voting Rights Act outlawed discriminatory voting practices. The Hart-Celler Bill was also passed in 1965, equalizing the national origins quota system under which immigrants from western Europe had historically been given preference. Because of this leveling, the Hart-Celler Act, though immigration legislation, was widely considered to be an extension of civil rights legislation.

It bears repeating that in 1965, on the heels of the Bracero Program (the massive contract worker program that brought an estimated five million workers from Mexico to the United States for temporary work), the Hart-Celler Act imposed quotas on legal entries from Latin America for the first time ever. Until this point, Latin American countries had been exempted from immigration quotas on the grounds that the labor of Mexican workers was essential for the U.S. economy. The new quotas capped Mexican immigration at levels far below the rate that had characterized Mexico–U.S. migration for several decades—in effect producing large-scale "illegal immigration" from Mexico. That is, at the same moment in history when African Americans were poised to enter the job market with legal equal rights, Mexican immigrant workers were being legally, but not actually, excluded from it. Immigration policy since the 1960s has been ever more oriented toward restriction and exclusion.

This should have been a boon to black workers, who would have been in a position to take advantage of employment opportunities created by the end of the Bracero Program and the imposition of immigration restrictions. But the economic circumstances of African Americans, instead of improving uniformly, have bifurcated since 1970. Although some African Americans did attain access to the middle class, poor and low-skill African Americans continue to be disproportionately excluded from the job market—and this is precisely the population that should have benefited most from immigration restrictions. In fact, according to the U.S. Census Bureau, more U.S. blacks are now concentrated in the lowest income category of under ten thousand dollars annually than in any other category.[10]

What happened? Why didn't the combination of civil rights legislation and restrictionist-oriented immigration legislation lead to better working and living conditions for most African Americans? The answer to this question is complex, but three major contributing factors can be identified: economic policy that allowed jobs to move abroad, immigration policy that "illegalized" but did not prevent large-scale immigration, and domestic policies that recast entire generations of urban minorities as criminal. Let us examine each in turn.

Economic policy that opened borders to trade and finance (while paradoxically closing them to workers) made it easier for U.S. businesses to move manufacturing abroad, where labor is cheaper. Attracted by abundant, low-paid, poorly protected labor in "developing" nations, many U.S. companies did just that, removing an important source of low-skill work from U.S. cities. This had a negative impact on the entire U.S. working class, including African American workers. But Steinberg (1995) points out that African Americans were more likely to be excluded from manufacturing jobs anyway, and it is unlikely that the loss of manufacturing is the sole or even the main cause of declining labor force participation rates among working-class African Americans. Furthermore, manufacturing jobs have been at least partially replaced in postindustrial areas by the expansion of the service sector, which has been identified in immigration scholarship as an important pull factor for immigrant labor flows. Ultimately, an increase in low-wage service work has not led to a corresponding increase in employment rates of African Americans. In spite of landmark civil rights legislation, African Americans have continued to face discrimination in the job market even when there are jobs to be had, leading Steinberg to conclude that "the nation [has] succumbed once again to its endemic racism, and to its collective indifference to the plight of its black citizens" (1995:95).

But an interpretation that attributes employment discrimination against African American workers to racism alone glosses over the economic dimension of racial segregation among low-wage workers. While persistent, personal anti-black racism against African Americans is one proximate cause for their continued exclusion from the labor market, employers' "racial preferences" also have a structural dimension: the appeal of an intensely powerless workforce. As Steinberg argues so eloquently elsewhere, racism is not reducible to personal or social beliefs that are "severed from the political and economic institutions" that maintain them. In fact, preferential hiring of immigrants over blacks is *not* due to racism alone, but to a *"clear preference* for foreign workers who are more *pliable and exploitable*, especially if they are undocumented" (1995:193; emphasis added). In the United States, a combination of border militarization and anti-immigrant policies has not reduced the flow of labor migration but has "illegalized" it, legitimizing exploitation of immigrant workers by making access to political, economic, and social resources a right of citizenship. If one "lesson of history is that blacks have overcome racist barriers in the occupational world only during periods when labor has been in tight supply" (Steinberg 1995:186), another lesson of history is that U.S. political policy is geared toward expanding vulnerable labor reserves, both immigrant and citizen. Legislation that illegalizes immigrants serves this end, as do policies that have incorporated entire generations of urban racial minorities into the criminal justice system.

In fact, at the same moment when African Americans should have been reaping the benefits of civil rights legislation, instead they were being incarcerated at unprecedented rates. Capitalizing on fear created by the agitations of the 1960s, legislators vowed to get "tough on crime" and introduced mandatory prison terms, long sentences, and increased penalties for narcotics violations. At a time when urban black communities were being ravaged by poverty and drugs, this campaign created a surge in the prison population in which African Americans were eight times more likely to be jailed than whites. Between 1970 and 2003, there was a sevenfold increase in the prison population in the United States, and by 2004, over 12 percent of African American men between the ages of 25 and 29 were behind bars.[11] Bruce Western (2006) views the prison boom as an escape valve for the increasing pressures caused by persistent unemployment and underemployment in postindustrial cities, as it simultaneously removed legions of unemployed African Americans from the streets and masked increasing poverty rates among African Americans in the cities.

Illegals and Criminals

As the scale of raids targeting undocumented immigrants has increased in the first decade of the twenty-first century, African

Americans *are* finding themselves working more as a result—as prisoners. In fact, employers facing a tight labor supply are not turning to empowered black workers to replace their undocumented labor force, but to prisoners, refugees, and homeless people. Labor shortages in the agricultural sector brought on by a reduction of the undocumented labor force have recently led growers to seek prison labor in both Colorado and Idaho.[12] In one telling example, a poultry-processing plant in Georgia lost two-thirds of its workforce in the aftermath of a 2006 immigration raid. According to a 2007 *Wall Street Journal* article, the plant raised wages and recruited local black workers to fill newly available jobs—a move that was initially touted as proof that labor shortages brought about by immigration enforcement would be a boon to black workers. But the honeymoon was short-lived; the new, predominantly African American workforce expressed concerns about dangerous work conditions and questionable labor practices at the plant, leading one manager to conclude that they simply "do not want to work." Rather than improve conditions and raise wages further, plant managers found new sources of pliant labor. They replaced their workforce once again—this time with prison workers, Hmong refugees, and homeless people.[13]

It seems as though, for these low-wage employers, "wanting to work" means either tolerating poor working conditions or being powerless to do anything about them. In fact, increasing concentrations of undocumented workers in low-wage, low-status jobs after 1970, and the continued exclusion of low-skilled black workers from the job market, are as much a function of powerlessness and its appeal to employers as they are a function of racism alone. In fact, political economic theories of labor migration suggest that the most important function of undocumented labor may not be its cheapness per se, but rather its inherent powerlessness.[14]

In sum, reserves of vulnerable low-wage labor in the United States have expanded, even in light of civil rights legislation and restrictionist immigration policy. This suggests that restrictionist immigration policies do not necessarily entail economic empowerment of African American workers; rather, white, African American, Asian, Latino, and other immigrant workers are marginalized at the same time by similar legislative trends. In fact, the proportion of immigrant workers characterized by illegal status has more than doubled since the 1970s, as has the proportion of U.S. workers in the criminal justice system.

Together, the undermining of workers' protections, the criminalization of immigrants and racial minorities, and the expansion of workfare programs has produced a steady supply of tractable and powerless labor in U.S. cities. Seen in this light, the criminalization of urban minorities and the illegalization of Latino immigrants increasingly serve much of the same function that race has historically served in the United States—at once rendering certain workers more vulnerable to oppressive labor practices and justifying such oppression with an idea of inherent inferiority. And while race and racism continue to function to preserve inequality, race is rarely invoked to *justify* inequality in formal political rhetoric. In an "Obama era," in which the United States is promoting itself as a nation of racial inclusion, the overtly racist tones of political discourse on labor are veiled, and illegality and criminality have become new *legitimate* bases for persistent exclusion and subordination.

Ultimately, Steinberg's hope that "immigration policy must take into account the legitimate interests of native workers, especially those on the economic margin" (201) is totally at odds with the demands of a flexible job market. It is protection of this market, not the interests of workers, that has been the primary concern of U.S. policy. There is no reason whatsoever to believe that racism or exploitation will be legislated away.

Moreover, as Nicholas De Genova (2005) argues, restricting immigration in the name of racial justice relegates race and racism in the United States to a black/white dichotomy in which Latino immigrants have no place. De Genova correctly points out—and Steinberg readily acknowledges—that the historical development of the U.S. economy has taken shape on the subjugated backs of both black *and* Mexican immigrant workers—as well as many others. By prioritizing the claims of citizen workers over Latin American immigrant workers, De Genova argues that Steinberg takes a nativist position that not only dehistoricizes the long-standing relationship of Mexican workers to U.S. society but denies its racist cast.

Legal restrictions on Latin American immigration have not led to economic empowerment of African Americans, and much less to the amelioration of institutionalized racism. In fact, anti-immigrant policy exacerbates racism and gives it fresh life. Fears and insecurities among the American working class are targeted by anti-immigrant groups eager to blame the decline of viable employment opportunities on immigrant workers. But this scapegoating only reinvents the idea that sociopolitical characteristics are a legitimate basis for distributing resources—in this case, the characteristic in question is putatively not race[15] but citizenship status; the resources—political rights and financial security—are the same. Like race, the assignment of illegal status to a segment of the workforce is a two-pronged attack that at once contributes to conditions of economic subordination and demeans a people in a profoundly personal way.

Toward an Anti-Nativist, Anti-Racist Perspective on Immigration

In spite of the evidence that U.S. policies have been complicit in constructing undocumented immigration from Mexico, some argue that exclusionary legislation should be upheld no matter the human cost. "The law is the law," restrictionists argue, and "illegal is illegal." But U.S. immigration policy, like all law, is social policy that develops from a particular history and is subject to change. At various times in U.S. history, women, African Americans, Asians, and white men who did not own property have been denied full citizenship rights in the United States. To cultivate a more just and inclusive society, native-born Americans and immigrants alike have struggled for progressive social change, "breaking" many laws along the way. This is why so many "criminals" of their day—George Washington, Harriet Tubman, and Rosa Parks, to name a few—have become heroes of the future.

And of course, laws are not merely determined by practical concerns but by humanitarian considerations as well. Part of the appeal of restrictionist rhetoric is that it is based on the idea that immigration status is a legitimate measure to determine whether a person should have access to resources like jobs and social services. But what makes citizenship status an accurate reflection of a person's worth? Most of us reject the idea that characteristics such as race, sexual orientation, religious affiliation, ethnicity, or even age are legitimate bases for excluding people from necessary resources. The acceptance of national origins, nation-state boundaries, and citizen/alien categories as bases for excluding people from resources naturalizes the political character of these distinctions and negates the meaningful ways in which unauthorized immigrants, legal immigrants, and U.S. citizens are members of the same globalized workforce.

Ultimately, the issues that are brought up by a theorization of undocumented labor migration—globalization, capitalism, racism, nativism, marginalization, class exploitation—are complex problems. And complex problems rarely have simple solutions. This is one reason, in a nutshell, why restricting immigration (even if such a measure were effective) would be unlikely to have a measurable long-term impact, beneficial or otherwise, on the well-being of U.S. citizen workers. Further, these problems are not only complex, they are international—created, transformed, and intensified by globalized interactions. International problems are not likely to have nationalist solutions. That is, inequality, exploitation, and uneven capitalist development will not be legislated away, even by the most well-intentioned policies. These complex global problems affect low-wage workers around the world in similar, if not equal, ways. Justice for workers will never be achieved by policies that accept racial, national, or legal divisions among the working class as legitimate bases on which to distribute resources. This means pushing beyond divisive perspectives that polarize the working class along racial, national, or legal lines, and taking an explicitly anti-racist, international stand.

Notes

1. Golash-Boza 2009; Lipman 2006.
2. Chacon and Davis 2006:165; Porter 2005.
3. Fonda 2006.
4. The anti-immigrant rhetoric of the Center for Immigration Studies has attracted the attention of the Southern Poverty Law Center (SPLC), a hate-group watchdog. The SPLC has posted the following about the CIS on their Web site: "Although the Center for Immigration Studies (CIS) bills itself as an 'independent' think tank that seeks 'to expand the base of public knowledge' about immigration, the Washington, D.C.-based group is only interested in one thing. CIS's reams of reports, as well as its blog postings, editorials, and frequent panels and press conferences, incessantly push the idea that America's immigration system is an unadulterated evil and that the only way to save America from impending doom is to cut drastically the number of immigrants. CIS has blamed immigrants, both legal and undocumented, for everything from terrorism to global warming. To make its case seem as strong as possible, CIS often manipulates data, relying on shaky statistics or faulty logic to come to the preordained conclusion that immigration is bad for this country. But CIS studies have been regularly debunked by mainstream academics and think tanks including the Immigration Policy Center, the Center for Budget and Policy Priorities and America's Voice." (www.splcenter.org/intel/nativist_cis.jsp)
5. Lipman 2006.
6. Annett 2006.
7. Tumulty 2006.
8. See Massey et al. 2002; Piore 1979; Sassen 1988.
9. Jefferson 2010; Neckerman and Kirshenman 1991; Waldinger and Lichter 2003.
10. U.S. Census Bureau 2007.
11. Western 2006:3.
12. Univision.com.
13. Perez and Dade 2007.
14. Portes and Walton 1981; Sassen 1988; Sassen-Koob 1981.
15. I say putatively not race because anti-immigrant sentiment and policy in the United States frequently have a racist cast in which immigrants who are not of European descent—Latinos, Asians, and Africans—are disproportionately stigmatized and subject to more restrictive immigration policies.

EPILOGUE

The Lions have experienced some significant changes in the more than six years that I have known them: some have become husbands, others have become fathers again, most have moved households. In this ethnography, I picked a static point in time—the inception of the research in the summer of 2007—and described the Lions' lives as they were then. Although this approach helps with clarity, it can give the false impression that the Lions' lives are static. This epilogue is designed to address that problem by providing a fuller description of the changes that have occurred in the Lions' lives from the fall of 2007 to the winter of early 2010.

Il Vino Buono

In 2008, Il Vino began to feel the squeeze of a contracting economy. In response to a slow but steady decline in business, the managers have cut back on product and personnel. The result appears to be an even sharper decline in business, as customers find that their favorite wine is no longer in stock, or that the bread is not as high-quality as they are used to, and many regular customers have found other places to eat. The entire service staff at Il Vino—including the busboys—is doubly impacted: they are working fewer hours and are making less in tips when they do work.

Alberto

The biggest change in Alberto's life happened without him: his youngest daughter was born. Just before her second birthday, in the spring of 2009, Alberto went back to Mexico—for good, he assured me. But only three months later, Alberto was back in Chicago and back at his busboy job at Il Vino. The economic situation in Mexico is bad, he says, and it is impossible for him to make a living there. He plans to continue to work at Il Vino and is making preliminary arrangements to bring his wife and daughters to the United States.

Alejandro

Alejandro has left his job at Uncle Luigi's to run his uncle's Mexican restaurant in a small town near Mokena, Illinois. The transition has not been easy. Even though he is in the position of general manager, he actually earns less income than he did as a busboy. He also laments the distance of his new job, since it has made it difficult for him to recruit Mexican workers; the staff that he manages is made up entirely of young white workers who, he says, don't have a stake in working hard. Alejandro remains with his long-term girlfriend, and he continues to spend weekends with his son.

Chuy

Chuy married his longtime girlfriend, who works as a teacher and serves on the weekends at Il Vino. He and Laica moved out of their apartment in Rene's house and into a nearby house that they purchased. They are consulting an attorney about the possibility of changing Chuy's legal status. Due to the housing slump, Chuy has lost his construction job and picked up three more shifts at Il Vino. He is using his new-found free time during the day to study English, and he hopes to return to construction work when the economy begins to grow again.

Lalo

Lalo went back to Mexico in the winter of 2007. I visited him at his house in León in the spring of 2008, where he seemed content to be at home with his wife and two younger sons (the oldest son remained in Chicago). He told me then that he was not planning to return to the United States, but in the fall of 2008 he called me from Texas looking for Roberto's phone number. He had managed to bring his entire family over the border, and they are currently living with his wife's siblings outside of Dallas, Texas.

Leonardo

After his demotion to daytime busboy, Leonardo kept a low profile among the Lions and spent more and more time with his girlfriend. In the winter of 2007, when Roberto left for Mexico, Leonardo and Roberto's apartment household split up. After a stint living with some distant relatives in the city's south side, Leonardo moved into the upstairs apartment at Rene's house that Chuy had vacated. After several months, Rene and Molly decided to join the two upstairs apartments into one, which suited the other family that lived upstairs because relatives of theirs had arrived from Mexico. Leonardo moved into a spare bedroom at Roberto's girlfriend's house. In the winter of 2008, his mother became seriously ill and went into a diabetic coma. Leonardo immediately left for Mexico and stayed there for three months, tending to his mom. Her health has improved, and Leonardo returned to Chicago in early spring 2009 (sponsored by Roberto). He brought his older brother, Juan, back with him. He has returned to Il Vino and is still working as a busboy.

Luis

Luis was fired from Il Vino in early fall, 2008, after failing to show up to work two days in a row without notice. He still lives with Alberto, Alejandro, and Carlos and, after a two-month period of unemployment, finally found another job as a busboy. He has been depressed and has started drinking heavily again and hanging out with his old friends. Although I lost touch with Luis, he called me in November of 2008 to ask me to bring a present to his mother in Mexico; unfortunately, I was already in León.

Manuel

Manuel has been the hardest hit by the economic contraction. He lost his rather high-paying construction job and continues to look for steady work. He found a job cleaning vents, but the irregular hours and low pay have prevented him from attaining financial security for his family. He has been teaming up with Luis and Chuy to work side jobs in construction, but the work is scarce. Finally, in the fall of 2009, Manuel and Liliana saved up enough money to move out of her parents' house and into a small rented home in the suburbs.

Omar

Omar continues to work in the kitchen at Uncle Luigi's and has been enjoying watching his daughter grow up. Unfortunately, things have not worked out between Omar and his wife, and he is currently staying with his brother Luis in the house that he shares with Alejandro and Alberto.

Rene

Rene and his wife, Molly, recently welcomed their third child. They continue to live in their home with the nice yard, and Rene is again the de facto head busboy at Il Vino. At Chuy's urging, Rene and Molly have been consulting an immigration attorney; they hope that an Obama presidency will bring changes in immigration law that will allow Rene to eventually adjust his legal status.

Roberto

One week before this book went to the publisher, I attended Roberto's going-away party—his second in two days. After five years, Roberto and his girlfriend decided to break up. Roberto moved in briefly with Manuel and his family, then went back to Mexico in the winter of early 2010. He is unsure whether this trip will amount to a brief vacation or turn into a permanent move, and he has no immediate plans to look for a job in León. Either way, he is excited about the prospect of seeing his family again and taking a break from his job at Il Vino. I asked Roberto about impending immigration reform, and whether he had considered that leaving at this time might jeopardize his chances at legalization—after more than ten years of working and living in the United States. "Yes," he told me, "I know, mi hija, but you know, that's life."

Interview Outline

Core Participants

Background

1. Where are you from, and what is it like there?
2. What was your family like?
3. Did you go to school? What did you study?
4. As you were growing up, was your father and/or mother employed, and if so, what did he or she do?
5. What work did your grandfather and/or grandmother do? What about your brothers and sisters?
6. Has your family lived for a long time in the place that you're from? If not, where did they live before, and why did they move?
7. Did you work at any jobs in the place that you're from? If so, what jobs? What was your income?

Migration

1. Why did you decide to emigrate to the United States?
2. Did you know anyone in the United States who helped you move? Did anyone in your family or any one of your friends support your decision to move?
3. How did you get into the United States?
4. How much did it cost you to move to the United States?
5. When you arrived in the United States where did you go?
6. What was your first job in the United States, and how did you get it?

Immigration and Legal Status

1. What was your legal status when you arrived in the United States?
2. What is your legal status currently, and if it has changed, how did it change?
3. How have you, as a Mexican immigrant, been treated by people in the United States?
4. Have you had any experiences in which you think you have been treated differently from a U.S. citizen because you are a Mexican immigrant?
5. Has there been any instance in which you feel like you have been taken advantage of or singled out because of your legal status?
6. Do you keep in contact with family and/or friends in Mexico? Do you send money to Mexico and, if so, how much? Have you gone back to Mexico since you first arrived in the United States?
7. Do you think that Mexican immigrants have a mostly positive or mostly negative impact on U.S. society? Please explain your answer.
8. Do you think that undocumented immigrants are criminals? Why or why not?
9. Have you helped a friend or relative cross the border and/or find work in the United States?

Work and Work Relations

1. Tell me about each job that you have had in the United States, including the type of work you did, how many hours per week you worked, how you got hired for the job, and how much you were paid.
2. For each of the jobs that you have had, how many of your co-workers were Mexican immigrants like yourself, and where were they from? Do you know what the legal status of your co-workers has been?
3. For each of your jobs, how many of your co-workers knew each other from "back home," or through friends from "back home"?
4. Would you say that, in general, the Mexican workers at the jobs that you have had help each other at work? Please explain your answer.
5. Do you think that being a Mexican immigrant affects the type of work you get and how much you get paid?
6. What were your non-Mexican co-workers like?
7. What have your employers been like?
8. How would you describe your relationships with your non-Mexican co-workers and employers?
9. Do you think you have ever been taken advantage of by an employer or co-worker because of your legal status?

10. Do you think that not having legal papers affects undocumented people's work relations and income? If so, in what ways?
11. Do you think you are a hard worker? Do you think that Mexicans as a group are hard working? Why or why not?
12. Have you worked with people who are not hard working, and if so, how have you and/or your co-workers handled that situation?
13. Do you have plans for work in the future?

Household Organization and Resources

1. Tell me about the places that you have lived in since you came to the United States, including who you lived with and what type of place (i.e. house, apartment, etc.) you lived in.
2. How did you meet the people that you have lived with? How did you come to live with them?
3. Have you shared bills with the people that you have lived with? How did you divide bills between household members and pay for them?
4. Have you shared household chores with the people that you have lived with? How did you decide who had which household responsibilities?
5. Have you pooled money with the people you have lived with?
6. Have you shared clothes, cars, or other things with people that you have lived with?
7. How have you and your housemates managed conflict between household members?

Identity and Community Solidarity

1. Describe the type of people who you think are most like you.
2. What things are most important to you in your life?
3. What characteristics do you most admire in your friends or family members?
4. Do you think that Mexican immigrants help each other out? If so, how?
5. Do you consider yourself part of a community? If so, what characteristics do members of your community have in common?
6. Are there any businesses that you know of that have policies or practices that help Mexican immigrants and people without legal papers? If so, what kinds of policies and practices are those?
7. Do you think that Mexicans as a group are different from other people? If so, how are they different?
8. Do you think that immigrants as a group are different from other people? If so, how?

Questions for Discussion

The following questions are intended to enrich students' reading of the book by promoting discussion and connecting some of the issues raised in the text with broader social science problems.

Chapter One

1. In the preface, I mention that I became friends with the Lions over the course of our acquaintance. Do you think that it is desirable for ethnographers to establish personal relationships with their study participants? Do friendships between ethnographer and participant enhance or diminish the quality of ethnographic research?

2. This ethnographic study took place just outside the city of Chicago—an area that is plagued by racial segregation and inequality. What do working-class, urban U.S. citizens have in common with undocumented immigrants like the Lions? In what ways are their situations meaningfully different?

Chapter Two

3. In this chapter, I point out that the U.S.–Mexico border was established by a war of conquest (and not, for example, by vote or mutual agreement). Should nation-states establish borders and control the movement of people over them? Who should get to decide such questions, and how?

4. This chapter presents historical material that shows how concepts of citizenship have shifted over time in relation to prevailing ideologies and needs in the United States. Do you think that there are parallels between the political exclusion of African-descended slaves in the United States—who formed a large segment of the U.S. workforce but were denied citizenship rights—and undocumented immigrants? How are the experiences of slaves and undocumented immigrants meaningfully similar? How are they meaningfully different?

Chapter Three

5. Among other things, this chapter examines how illegal status makes the Lions vulnerable and contributes to their marginalization. How does this affect our understanding of workers' agency? To what degree are poor, disenfranchised, or otherwise marginalized people able to affect their world? How is their agency limited? Is it appropriate to speak of meaningful human agency among people who have very little political or economic power?

6. Many Mexican workers like the Lions are not driven to migrate by extreme poverty but rather by a host of social and economic considerations. Do you agree with their Mexican family members that decisions to migrate without authorization are morally justified, or are you inclined to agree with those who believe that there is no justifiable reason for breaking immigration law? What kinds of criteria would you use to examine this question?

Chapter Four

7. Anthropologists have traditionally studied small-scale, non-Western "cultures." Increasingly, anthropologists of globalization have focused on the interconnections between groups of people around the world and particularly on how "cultures" themselves are being continuously created within broader political, economic, and social landscapes. Do the Lions have a "culture"? If so, is it different from Mexican culture? Is it different from American culture?

8. In the absence of their families and without the support of a broader community, the Lions became very reliant on each other for material and nonmaterial resources. In essence, friendships became very important for them. Are there parallels between the Lions' social networks and those of other alienated or isolated social groups that you can think of?

Chapter Five

9. When they work, the Lions remind me of a competitive team in which members pressure each other to perform. In what other situations

are individuals encouraged or pressured to conform to group expectations? What are the advantages of belonging to a group or team? What are the drawbacks?

10. At the end of this chapter, I argue that insofar as the Lions reproduce racialized perceptions of their labor, they perpetuate categorical inequalities that ultimately constrain them. Do you agree with this conclusion? Do you think that by working really hard, the Lions become complicit in their own subordination?

Chapter Six

11. In their conversations about race, the Lions both reproduce and resist racial stereotypes of themselves and others. What are racial stereotypes, and how do they function? What impact do stereotypes about Mexican workers have on the Lions' behaviors and their social identities?

12. When I asked the Lions to rate the things that were most important in their lives, only Alberto gave religion a high rating (although they all self-identify as Catholic). Is this consistent with other things that you have heard or read about Mexicans and Mexican culture? What are some possible explanations for the relative lack of importance of religion in the Lions' lives?

Chapter Seven

13. In the United States, we tend to think of incarceration as a logical and justifiable response to a person's having committed a crime. In this chapter, I present the argument that the proportional expansion of the incarcerated population in the U.S. has to do with changes in criminal legislation that disproportionately affected racial minorities, and I hypothesize that these policies are similar to those that have "illegalized" immigrants. What are the strengths and weaknesses of this argument? How can it be evaluated?

14. In this chapter, I mention but do not discuss in depth the idea that the anti-immigrant movement is racist. Is it? How can we tell?

15. If it could be shown that deporting all undocumented immigrants would have an overall beneficial impact on U.S. citizens, should it be done? Who should get to decide, and on what grounds?

Suggestions for Further Reading

Alvarez, Roberto. 2005. *Mangos, Chiles and Truckers: The Business of Transnationalism.* Minneapolis: University of Minnesota Press.

Chang, Grace. 2000. *Disposable Domestics: Immigrant Women Workers in the Global Economy.* Cambridge, MA: South End Press.

Chavez, Leo R. 1992. *Shadowed Lives: Undocumented Immigrants in American Society.* New York: Wadsworth.

Cohen, Jeffrey H. 2004. *The Culture of Migration in Southern Mexico.* Austin: University of Texas Press.

De Genova, Nicholas. 2005. *Working the Boundaries: Race, Space, and "Illegality" in Mexican Chicago.* Durham, NC: Duke University Press.

De Genova, Nicholas, and Ana Y. Ramos-Zayas. 2003. *Latino Crossings: Mexicans, Puerto Ricans, and the Politics of Race and Citizenship.* New York: Routledge.

Fernandez-Kelly, Maria Patricia. 1983. *For We Are Sold, I and My People: Women and Industry in Mexico's Frontier.* Albany: University of New York Press.

Fine, Gary Alan. 1996. *Kitchens: The Culture of Restaurant Work.* Berkeley: University of California Press.

Hondagneu-Sotelo, Pierrette. 2001. *Doméstica: Immigrant Workers Cleaning and Caring in the Shadows of Affluence.* Berkeley: University of California Press.

Massey, Douglas, Jorge Durand, and Nolan J. Malone. 2002. *Beyond Smoke and Mirrors: Mexican Immigration in an Era of Economic Integration.* New York: Russell Sage Foundation.

Ngai, Mae. 2004. *Impossible Subjects: Illegal Aliens and the Making of Modern America.* Princeton, NJ: Princeton University Press.

Pribilsky, Jason. 2007. *La Chulla Vida: Gender, Migration, and the Family in Andean Ecuador and New York City.* New York: Syracuse University Press.

Romero, Mary. 2002. *Maid in the U.S.A.* New York: Routledge.

Smith, Robert C. 2006. *Mexican New York: Transnational Lives of New Immigrants.* Berkeley: University of California Press.

Stephen, Lynn. 2007. *Transborder Lives: Indigenous Oaxacans in Mexico, California, and Oregon.* Durham, NC: Duke University Press.

Vila, Pablo. 2000. *Crossing Borders, Reinforcing Borders: Social Categories, Metaphors, and Narrative Identities on the U.S.–Mexico Frontier.* Austin: University of Texas Press.

Waldinger, Roger, and Michael Lichter. 2003. *How the Other Half Works: Immigration and the Social Organization of Labor.* Berkeley: University of California Press.

Zlolniski, Christian. 2006. *Janitors, Street Vendors, and Activists: The Lives of Mexican Immigrants in Silicon Valley.* Berkeley: University of California Press.

Glossary of Spanish Terms

El Bajío. A region in north-central Mexico that encompasses parts of the states of Guanajuato, Michoacán, and Querétaro. The Bajío is known for its agricultural productivity and also as a historical "sending" region of workers to the United States.

barbero. "Suck-up" or "kiss-ass"; the Lions use the term "barbero" disparagingly to distance themselves from workers who gain job security by sucking-up to the boss.

bracero. A temporary contract worker from Mexico who worked as part of the Bracero Program (1949–1964), a binational pact for the massive importation of Mexican workers to the United States.

coyote. A people smuggler; undocumented workers use coyotes to pass them over the border without authorization.

echándole ganas. "Putting your back into it"; the Lions use the phrase "echándole ganas" to describe how they work hard (as opposed to barberos).

ejido. A communally held parcel of land. The ejido system has a long history in Mesoamerica, but it largely disappeared during the colonial period. Land reform measures instituted after the Mexican Revolution (1910–1917) reestablished the widespread use of ejidos, which are often divided into family holdings like that of Papa Juan.

gabacho. "White guy."

ganarle al patrón. "Win the boss"; the Lions emphasize the importance of winning over the boss to gain security and respect on the job.

mojarones. "Wetbacks"; derived from *mojado*, which means "wet." The Lions often refer to themselves and other Mexican workers as "mojarones." While the Lions use the term jokingly, they are acutely aware of its derogatory connotations and did not want me to emphasize their usage of the term in this book.

superarse. "Get ahead" or "improve oneself"; the Lions emphasize their desire to *superarse* or improve themselves when they talk about their reasons for migrating without authorization.

Glossary of English Terms

capital. In its most basic usage, capital is a form of wealth that produces more wealth; capital often takes the form of productive machinery, such as factory equipment or agricultural equipment, and usually takes substantial financial assets to acquire. For the Lions' fathers and grandfathers, finding wage work was important to buy capital, such as tractors, plows, and irrigation equipment, to invest in their farmland in order to make it productive.

ICE. Immigration and Customs Enforcement, an agency in the Department of Homeland Security (created in 2003) that is responsible for enforcement of U.S. immigration policy.

Immigration Act of 1965. Also known as the Hart-Celler Act, equalized national quotas on immigration, placing numerical restrictions on legal immigration from Western Hemisphere countries (including Mexico) for the first time.

IIRAIRA. The Illegal Immigration Reform and Immigrant Responsibility Act of 1996. IIRAIRA was restrictionist-oriented immigration legislation that, among other things, substantially increased the buildup of enforcement measures on the border, increased penalties for smugglers and undocumented people, limited public benefits that immigrants could receive, made it easier to deport immigrants, and made it more difficult for immigrants to adjust their legal status.

IMF. The International Monetary Fund, one of two international institutions (the World Bank is the other) whose main function is to provide loans to developing nations. While the IMF is ostensibly not affiliated with any particular nation-state, its creation and management has been particularly influenced by the United States and Great Britain, and there is broad agreement among social science scholars that the IMF and the World Bank promote the interests of Western capitalists in developing nations, particularly by "encouraging" them to adopt neoliberal policies.

INS. Immigration and Naturalization Service, an agency of the United States Department of Justice that handled immigration-related issues between 1870 and 2003. In 2003 the functions of the INS were transferred to various agencies—including ICE—in the newly created Department of Homeland Security.

IRCA. The Immigration Reform and Control Act of 1986. IRCA is most known for two provisions: sanctions against employers who can be proven to have knowingly employed undocumented workers, and an amnesty program under which nearly three million undocumented people legalized their status.

militarization. The buildup of military resources in an area. In migration scholarship, militarization often refers to the establishment of walls, fences, surveillance equipment, and military or police personnel along a border region.

nativism. Feelings of primacy or superiority toward the established residents of a region ("natives"), typically associated with opposition to immigration, newcomers, or anyone perceived as foreign.

neoliberalism. An approach to political economy that favors deregulation and privatization of business in the promotion of a free-market system. Neoliberalism tends to be associated with contemporary globalization because it promotes unfettered economic relationships over nation-state borders and loosens or abolishes national and regional economic systems.

norms. Shared, understood rules of behavior.

Operation Gatekeeper. Initiated in 1994, Operation Gatekeeper was a security operation designed to prevent migrant crossings between Tijuana and San Diego. Operation Gatekeeper symbolizes the beginning of a series of military-style operations along the U.S.–Mexico border during the 1990s that have not stopped unauthorized crossings but have made them more dangerous and expensive.

Operation Wetback. Initiated in 1954, Operation Wetback was an organized effort by the United States government to arrest and deport undocumented Mexican workers, many of whom were subsequently processed as bracero workers and sent back to work in the United States.

remittances. Money that is sent from one place to another; in the context of migration, remittances usually refer to money that migrants working abroad send back to family members in their communities of origin.

social identity. The identification of people with certain social categories or groups and their disassociation from others; the Lions, for example, cultivate social identities as hard workers and draw boundaries against people whom they perceive as lazy, opportunistic, or selfish.

social network. An interconnected group of people with relationships of interdependency.

transnational. An adjective that can refer to any relationship that spans nation-state boundaries; scholars of migration frequently refer to transnational migration and transnational social networks to describe the social, economic, and political relationships among people in different nations.

World Bank. See IMF.

REFERENCES CITED

Adler, Rachel. 2005. Oye Comprade! The Chef Needs a Dishwasher: Yucatecan Men in the Dallas Restaurant Economy. *Urban Anthropology* 34 (2–3): 217–246.

Annett, Tim. 2006. Illegal Immigrants and the Economy. *Wall Street Journal.* April 13.

Appadurai, Arjun. 1996. *Modernity at Large: Cultural Dimensions of Globalization.* Minneapolis: University of Minnesota Press.

———. 2004. The Capacity to Aspire: Culture and the Terms of Recognition. In *Culture and Public Action,* ed. Vijayendra Rao and Michael Walton, pp. 59–84. Delhi: Permanent Black.

Arias, Patricia. 2004. Old Paradigms and New Scenarios in a Migratory Tradition: U.S. Migration from Guanajuato. In *Crossing the Border: Research from the Mexican Migration Project,* ed. Jorge Durand and Douglas Massey, pp. 171–183. New York: Russell Sage Foundation.

Basch, Linda, Nina Glick Schiller, and Cristina Szanton Blanc. 1994. *Nations Unbound: Transnational Projects, Postcolonial Predicaments, and Deterritorialized Nation-States.* Amsterdam: Gordon and Breach Science Publishers.

Bashi Bobb, Vilna. 2001. Neither Ignorance nor Bliss: Race, Racism, and the West Indian Experience. In *Migration, Transnationalization, and Race in a Changing New York,*. ed. Hector Cordero-Guzman, Robert C. Smith, and Ramon Grosfoguel., pp. 212–238. Philadelphia: Temple University Press.

Bourgois, Philippe. 2003 [1996]. *In Search of Respect: Selling Crack in El Barrio,* 2nd ed. New York: Cambridge University Press.

Brodkin, Karen. 2007. *Making Democracy Matter: Identity and Activism in Los Angeles.* New Brunswick, NJ: Rutgers University Press.

Burawoy, Michael. 1979. *Manufacturing Consent: Changes in the Labor Process under Monopoly Capitalism.* Chicago: University of Chicago Press.

Calavita, Kitty. 1994. U.S. Immigration and Policy Responses: the Limits of Legislation. In *Controlling Immigration*, ed. Wayne Cornelius, Philip Martin, and James Hollifield, pp. 55–82. Stanford, CA: Stanford University Press.

Camarota, Steven. 2004. The High Cost of Cheap Labor: Illegal Immigration and the Federal Budget. Washington D.C.: Center for Immigration Studies. http://www.cis.org/node/54 (Accessed October 3, 2009).

Campo-Flores, Arian. 2006. America's Divide. *Newsweek*. April 10.

Cardoso, Lawrence A. 1980. *Mexican Emigration to the United States 1987–1931*. Tucson: University of Arizona Press.

Centeno, Miguel, Sara Curran, John Galloway, Paulette Lloyd, Suresh Sood, and Abigail Cooke. 2005. *The Rise of NAFTA*. Princeton, NJ: Center for Migration and Development. http://www.princeton.edu/~ina/gkg/ (Accessed March 7, 2006).

Cerrutti, Marcela, and Douglas Massey. 2004. Trends in Mexican Migration to the United States, 1965 to 1995. In *Crossing the Border: Research from the Mexican Migration Project*, ed. Jorge Durand and Douglas Massey, pp. 17–44. New York: Russell Sage Foundation.

Chacon, Justin, and Mike Davis. 2006. *No One is Illegal: Fighting Racism and State Violence on the U.S.-Mexico Border*. Chicago: Haymarket Books.

Chasteen, John. 2006. *Born in Blood and Fire: A Concise History of Latin America*, 2nd ed. New York: W. W. Norton & Company.

Chang, Grace. 2000. *Disposable Domestics: Immigrant Women Workers in the Global Economy*. Cambridge: South End Press.

Chavez, Leo R. 1992. *Shadowed Lives: Undocumented Immigrants in American Society*. New York: Wadsworth.

Cohen, Jeffrey H. 2001. Transnational Migration in Rural Oaxaca, Mexico: Dependency, Development, and the Household. *American Anthropologist* 103 (4): 954–967.

———. 2004. *The Culture of Migration in Southern Mexico*. Austin: University of Texas Press.

Conover, Ted. 1987. *Coyotes: A Journey through the Secret World of America's Illegal Aliens*. New York: Random House Publishing.

Cornelius, Wayne. 1989. Impacts of the 1986 US Immigration Law on Emigration from Rural Mexican Sending Communities. *Population and Development Review* 15:689–705.

Cornelius, Wayne, and Philip Martin. 1993. The Uncertain Connection: Free Trade and Rural Mexican Migration to the United States. *International Migration Review* 27:484–512.

Coutin, Susan Bibler, and Phyllis Pease Chock. 1997. "Your Friend, the Illegal": Definition and Paradox in Newspaper Accounts of U.S. Immigration Reform. *Identities* 2 (1–2): 123–148.

DeFreitas, Gregory. 1995. *Immigration, Inequality, and Policy Alternatives*. New York: Russell Sage Foundation. http://epn.org/sage/rsdefr.html (Accessed October 3, 2009).

De Genova, Nicholas. 2005. *Working the Boundaries: Race, Space, and "Illegality" in Mexican Chicago*. Durham, NC: Duke University Press.

De Genova, Nicholas, and Ana Y. Ramos-Zayas. 2003. *Latino Crossings: Mexicans, Puerto Ricans, and the Politics of Race and Citizenship*. New York: Routledge.

di Leonardo, Micaela. 1998. *Exotics at Home: Anthropologies, Others, and American Modernity*. Chicago: University of Chicago Press.

Douglas, Mary. 2004. Traditional Culture—Let's Hear No More About It. In *Culture and Public Action*, ed. Vijayendra Rao and Michael Walton, pp. 85–109. Delhi: Permanent Black.

Fernandez-Kelly, Maria Patricia. 1983. *For We Are Sold, I and My People: Women and Industry in Mexico's Frontier*. Albany: State University of New York Press.

Fine, Gary Alan. 1996. *Kitchens: The Culture of Restaurant Work*. Berkeley: University of California Press.

Fonda, Daren. 2006. What It Means for Your Wallet. *Time*, April 5.

Fragomen Jr., Austin. 1997. The Illegal Immigration Reform and Immigrant Responsibility Act of 1996: An Overview. *International Migration Review* 31 (2): 438–460.

Fussell, Elizabeth. 2004. Sources of Mexico's Migration Stream: Rural, Urban, and Border Migrants to the United States. *Social Forces* 82:927–967.

Gamio, Manuel. 1971 [1930]. *Mexican Immigration to the United States: A Study of Human Migration and Adjustment*. New York: Dover Publications, Inc.

Garcia, Carlos. 2005. Buscando Trabajo: Social Networking among Immigrants from Mexico to the United States. *Hispanic Journal of Behavioral Sciences* 27:3–22.

Gershon, Ilana, and Janelle S. Taylor. 2008. Introduction to "In Focus: Culture in the Spaces of No Culture." *American Anthropologist* 110 (4): 417–421.

Giddens, Anthony. 1993. Problems of Action and Structure. In *The Giddens Reader*, ed. Philip Cassell, pp. 88–175. Stanford: Stanford University Press.

Goffman, Erving. 1959. *The Presentation of Self in Everyday Life*. New York: Anchor Books.

Golash-Boza, Tanya . 2009. A Confluence of Interests in Immigration Enforcement: How Politicians, the Media, and Corporations Profit from Immigration Policies Destined to Fail. *Sociology Compass* 3 (2009): 293–294.

Gomberg, Paul. 2007. *How to Make Opportunity Equal: Race and Contributive Justice*. Malden, MA: Blackwell.

Gomberg-Muñoz, Ruth. 2010. Willing to Work: Agency and Vulnerability in an Undocumented Immigrant Network. *American Anthropologist* 112 (2):295–307.

Gorman, Anna. 2005. Employers of Illegal Immigrants Face Little Risk of Penalty. *Los Angeles Times,* May 29.

Gray, Mia. 2004. The social construction of the service sector: Institutional structures and labour market outcomes. *Geoforum* 35 (2004): 23–34.

Greider, William. 1997. *One World, Ready or Not: The Manic Logic of Global Capitalism*. New York: Simon & Schuster.

Gunewardena, Nandini, and Ann Kingsolver. 2007. Introduction. In *The Gender of Globalization: Women Navigating Cultural and Economic Marginalization*, ed. Nandini Gunewardena and Ann Kingsolver, pp. 3–21. Santa Fe, NM: School for Advanced Research Press.

Gupta, Akhil, and James Ferguson. 1997. Discipline and Practice: "The Field" as Site, Method, and Location in Anthropology. In *Anthropological Locations: Boundaries and Grounds of a Field Science*, ed. Akhil Gupta and James Ferguson, pp. 1–46. Berkeley: University of California Press.

Gutierrez, David G.. 1995. *Walls and Mirrors: Mexican Americans, Mexican Immigrants, and the Politics of Ethnicity*. Berkeley: University of California Press.

Gutmann, Matthew. 2007. *The Meanings of Macho: Being a Man in Mexico City*. Berkeley: University of California Press.

Harvey, David. 2005. *A Brief History of Neoliberalism*. New York: Oxford University Press.

Heyman, Josiah. 1998. State Effects on Labor Exploitation: The INS and undocumented immigrants at the Mexico-United States border. *Critique of Anthropology* 18 (2): 157–180.

———. 2001. Class and Classification at the U.S.-Mexico Border. *Human Organization* 60 (2): 128–140.

Hondagneu-Sotelo, Pierrette. 1994. *Gendered Transitions: Mexican Experiences of Immigration*. Berkeley: University of California Press.

———. 2001. *Doméstica: Immigrant Workers Cleaning and Caring in the Shadows of Affluence*. Berkeley: University of California Press.

Jefferson, Cord. 2010. How Illegal Immigration Hurts Black America. *The Root*. http://www.theroot.com/views/how-illegal-immigration-hurts-black-america (Accessed October 3, 2009).

Jimenez, Maria. 2009. Humanitarian Crisis: Migrant Deaths at the U.S.–Mexico Border. San Diego: ACLU of San Diego & Imperial Counties and Mexico's National Commission of Human Rights. http://www.aclusandiego.org/article_downloads/000888/Humanitarian%20Crisis%20Report%209-30-09.pdf (Accessed December 20, 2009).

Kearney, Michael. 2004. The Classifying and Value-Filtering Missions of Borders. *Anthropological Theory* 4 (2): 131–156.

Kirkwood, Burton. 2000. *The History of Mexico*. New York: Palgrave.

Kochhar, Rakesh. 2005. *Survey of Mexican Migrants, Part Three: The Economic Transition to America*. Washington, DC: Pew Hispanic Center. http://pewhispanic.org/reports/report.php?ReportID=58 (Accessed May 12, 2007).

Krauze, Enrique. 1997. *Mexico: Biography of Power*. New York: Harper Perennial.

Lamont, Michele. 2000. *The Dignity of Working Men: Morality and the Boundaries of Race, Class, and Immigration*. Russell Sage Foundation: New York.

Lipman, Francine. 2006. The Taxation of Undocumented Immigrants: Separate, Unequal, and Without Representation. *Harvard Latino Law Review* 9:1–58.

Lipsitz, George . 2005. Foreword. In *Mangos, Chiles and Truckers: the Business of Transnationalism*, by Robert Alvarez. Minneapolis: University of Minnesota Press.

MacLeod, Jay. 1995 [1987]. *Ain't No Makin' It: Aspirations and Attainment in a Low-Income Neighborhood*. Boulder, CO: Westview Press.

Maiello, Michael, and Nicole Ridgway. 2006. Alien Nation. *Forbes*. April 10.

Marx, Karl. 1973 [1852]. The Eighteenth Brumaire of Louis Bonaparte. In *Surveys from Exile: Political Writings, Vol. 2.*, ed. David Fernbach, pp.143–249. New York: Penguin Books.

Massey, Douglas. 1988. Economic Development and International Migration in Comparative Perspective. *Population and Development Review* 14:383–413.

Massey, Douglas, Joaquin Arango, Graeme Hugo, Ali Kouaouchi, Adela Pellegrino, and J. Edward Taylor. 1994. An Evaluation of International Migration Theory: The North American Case. *Population and Development Review* 20:699–751.

Massey, Douglas, Jorge Durand, and Nolan J. Malone. 2002. *Beyond Smoke and Mirrors: Mexican Immigration in an Era of Economic Integration*. New York: Russell Sage Foundation.

Mehta, Chirag, Nik Theodore, Iliana Mora, and Jennifer Wade. 2002. *Chicago's Undocumented Immigrants: An Analysis of Wages, Working Conditions, and Economic Contributions*. Chicago: UIC Center for Urban Economic Development.

Menchaca, Martha, and Richard Valencia. 1990. Anglo-Saxon Ideologies in the 1920s–1930s: Their Impact on the Segregation of Mexican Students in California. *Anthropology & Education Quarterly* 21:222–249.

Moss, Philip, and Chris Tilly. 2001. *Stories Employers Tell: Race, Skill, and Hiring in America*. New York: Russell Sage Foundation.

Nagel, Joane. 1994. Constructing ethnicity: Creating and recreating ethnic identity and culture. *Social Problems* 41:152–176.

Neckerman, Kathryn, and Joleen Kirschenman. 1991. Hiring Strategies, Racial Bias, and Inner City Workers. *Social Problems* 38 (4): 433–447.

Ngai, Mae. 2004. *Impossible Subjects: Illegal Aliens and the Making of Modern America*. Princeton, NJ: Princeton University Press.

Omi, Michael, and Howard Winant. 1994. *Racial Formation in the United States from the 1960s to the 1990s*. New York: Routledge.

Orrenius, Pia. 2004. The Effect of U.S. Border Enforcement on the Crossing Behavior of Mexican Migrants. In *Crossing the Border: Research from the Mexican Migration Project*, eds. Jorge Durand and Douglas Massey, pp. 281–298. New York: Russell Sage Foundation.

Ortner, Sherry. 1997. Thick Resistance: Death and the Cultural Construction of Agency in Himalayan Mountaineering, in *The Fate of "Culture": Geertz and Beyond*, Special issue, *Representations* 59:135–162.

———. 2006. *Anthropology and Social Theory: Culture, Power, and the Acting Subject*. Durham, NC: Duke University Press.

Passel, Jeffrey. 2006. *Size and Characteristics of the Unauthorized Migrant Population in the U.S.: Estimates Based on the March 2005 Current Population Survey.* Washington DC: Pew Hispanic Center. http://pewhispanic.org/reports/report.php?ReportID=61 (accessed November 1, 2009).

Passel, Jeffrey, and D'Vera Cohn. 2009. *A Portrait of Unauthorized Immigration in the United States.* Washington DC: Pew Hispanic Center. http://pewhispanic.org/files/reports/107.pdf (accessed August 13, 2009).

Pedraza, Silvia, and Ruben G. Rumbaut. 1996. *Origins and Destinies: Immigration, Race, and Ethnicity in America.* New York: Wadsworth Publishing Company.

Perez, Evan, and Corey Dade. 2007. Reversal of Fortune: An Immigration Raid Aids Blacks–For a Time. *Wall Street Journal.* (Eastern Edition). January 17.

Pew Hispanic Center. 2006a. *Recently Arrived Migrants and the Congressional Debate on Immigration.* Washington, DC: Author. http://pewhispanic.org/files/factsheets/15.pdf (Accessed July 20, 2007).

———. 2006b. *The State of American Public Opinion on Immigration in Spring 2006.* Washington, DC: Author. http://pewhispanic.org/factsheets/factsheet.php?FactsheetID=18 (Accessed July 20. 2007).

———. 2007. *National Survey of Latinos: As Illegal Immigration Issue Heats Up, Hispanics Feel a Chill.* Washington, DC: Author. http://pewhispanic.org/reports/report.php?ReportID=84 (accessed December 12, 2008).

———. 2009. *Statistical Portrait of the Foreign-Born Population in the United States, 2007.* Washington, DC: Author. http://pewhispanic.org/factsheets/factsheet.php?FactsheetID=45 (Accessed December 17, 2009).

Piore, Michael. 1979. *Birds of Passage: Migrant Labor and Industrial Societies.* New York: Cambridge University Press.

Plascencia, Luis. 2009. The "Undocumented" Mexican Migrant Question: Re-Examining the Framing of Law and Illegalization in the United States. *Urban Anthropology* 38 (2–4):376–434.

Porter, Eduardo. 2005. Illegal Immigrants Are Bolstering Social Security with Billions. *New York Times,* April 5.

———. 2006a. The Search for Illegal Immigrants Stops at the Workplace. *New York Times,* March 5.

———. 2006b. Here Illegally, Working Hard and Paying Taxes. *New York Times,* June 19.

Portes, Alejandro, and Patricia Landolt. 2000. Social Capital: Promises and Pitfalls of Its Role in Development. *Journal of Latin American Studies* 32:529–547.

Portes, Alejandro, and Ruben Rumbaut. 1996. *Immigrant America: A Portrait.* Berkeley: University of California Press.

Portes, Alejandro, and John Walton. 1981. *Labor, Class, and the International System.* New York: Academic Press.

Preston, Julia. 2006. Pickers Are Few, and Growers Blame Congress. *New York Times,* September 22.

Preston, Julia, and Samuel Dillon. 2004. *Opening Mexico: The Making of a Democracy.* New York: Farrar, Straus and Giroux.

Pribilsky, Jason. 2007. *La Chulla Vida: Gender, Migration, and the Family in Andean Ecuador and New York City.* Syracuse, NY: Syracuse University Press.

Rao, Vijayendra, and Michael Walton. 2004. Culture and Public Action: Relationality, Equality of Agency, and Development. In *Culture and Public Action,* ed. Vijayendra Rao and Michael Walton, pp. 3–36. Delhi: Permanent Black.

Ready, Timothy, and Allert Brown-Gort. 2005. *The State of Latino Chicago: This Is Home Now.* Notre Dame, IN: University of Notre Dame, Institute for Latino Studies. http://latinostudies.nd.edu/pubs/pubs/StateofLatino-final.pdf (accessed July 10, 2007).

Roberts, Kenneth D. 1982. Agrarian Structure and Labor Mobility in Rural Mexico. *Population and Development Review* 8:299–322.

Romero, Mary. 2002. *Maid in the U.S.A.* New York: Routledge.

Rosenblatt, Daniel. 2004. An Anthropology Made Safe for Culture: Patterns of Practice and the Politics of Difference in Ruth Benedict. *American Anthropologist* 106 (3): 459–472.

Sassen, Saskia. 1988. *The Mobility of Labor and Capital: A Study in International Investment and Labor Flow.* Cambridge: Cambridge University Press.

Sassen-Koob, Saskia. 1981. Towards a Conceptualization of Immigrant Labor. *Social Problems* 29 (1): 65–85.

Sen, Amartya. 2004. How Does Culture Matter? In *Culture and Public Action,* ed. Vijayendra Rao and Michael Walton, pp. 37–58. Delhi: Permanent Black.

Sewell, William H. 1992. A Theory of Structure: Duality, Agency, and Transformation. *The American Journal of Sociology* 98 (1): 1–29

Smith, Robert C. 2006. *Mexican New York: Transnational Lives of New Immigrants.* Berkeley: University of California Press.

Smith-Nonini, Sandy. 2007. Sticking to the Union: Anthropologists and "Union Maids" in San Francisco. In *The Gender of Globalization: Women Navigating Cultural and Economic Marginalization,* ed. Nandini Gunewardena and Ann Kingsolver, pp. 197–214. Santa Fe, NM: School for Advanced Research Press.

Steinberg, Stephen. 1995. *Turning Back: The Retreat from Racial Justice in American Thought and Policy.* Boston: Beacon Press.

———. 2005. Immigration, African Americans, and Race Discourse. *New Politics.* http://www.wpunj.edu/~newpol/issue39/Steinberg39.htm (accessed August 13, 2009).

Stephen, Lynn. 2007. *Transborder Lives: Indigenous Oaxacans in Mexico, California, and Oregon.* Durham, NC: Duke University Press.

Stepick, Alex, and Guillermo Grenier, with Hafidh A. Hafidh, Sue Chaffee, and Debbie Draznin. 1994. The View from the Back of the House: Restaurants and Hotels in Miami. In *Newcomers in the Workplace: Immigrants and the Restructuring of the U.S. Economy,* ed. Louise Lamphere, Alex Stepick, and Guillermo Grenier, pp. 181–198. Philadelphia: Temple University Press.

Suarez-Orozco, Carola, and Marcelo Suarez-Orozco. 1995. *Transformations: Immigration, Family Life, and Achievement Motivation Among Latino Adolescents.* Stanford, CA: University of Stanford Press.

Suro, Roberto, and Gabriel Escobar. 2006. *2006 National Survey of Latinos: The Immigration Debate.* Washington, DC: Pew Hispanic Center. http://pewhispanic.org/reports/report.php?ReportID=68 (Accessed July 20. 2007).

Swarns, Rachel L. 2006. Growing Effort to Influence U.S. Policy. *New York Times.* April 11.

Tilly, Charles. 1998. *Durable Inequality.* Berkeley: University of California Press.

Tumulty, Karen. 2006. Should They Stay or Should They Go? *Time.* April 10.

U.S. Census Bureau. 2007. Statistical Abstract of the United States. Table 689. Money Income of People—Number by Income Level and by Sex, Race, and Hispanic Origin. http://www.census.gov/compendia/statab/2010/tables/10s0689.pdf (Accessed February 12, 2010).

Univision.com. 2009. *A falta de inmigrantes, reclusos: Escasez de campesinos en campos de Idaho.* [When Immigrants are Scarce, Prisoners: A Shortage of Farmworkers in the Fields of Idaho.] http://www.univision.com/content/content.jhtml?cid=1226109# (Accessed December 31, 2009).

Urbina, Ian. 2009. After Pennsylvania Trial, Tensions Simmer Over Race. *New York Times,* May 16.

Valenzuela Jr., Abel, Nik Theodore, Edwin Melendez, and Ana Luz Gonzalez. 2006. *On the Corner: Day Labor in the United States.* www.sscnet.ucla.edu/issr/csup/index.php (Accessed July 20, 2007).

Vila, Pablo. 2000. *Crossing Borders, Reinforcing Borders: Social Categories, Metaphors, and Narrative Identities on the U.S.-Mexico Frontier.* Austin: University of Texas Press.

Waldinger, Roger, and Michael Lichter. 2003. *How the Other Half Works: Immigration and the Social Organization of Labor.* Berkeley: University of California Press.

Waters, Mary. 1990. *Ethnic Options: Choosing Identities in America.* Berkeley: University of California Press.

Weaver, Frederick Stirton. 2000. *Latin America in the World Economy: Mercantile Colonialism to Global Capitalism.* Boulder, CO: Westview Press.

Western, Bruce. 2006. *Punishment and Inequality in America.* New York: Russell Sage Foundation.

Willis, Paul. 1977. *Learning to Labor: How working class kids get working class jobs.* New York: Columbia University Press.

Zlolniski, Christian. 2003. Labor Control and Resistance of Mexican Immigrant Janitors in Silicon Valley. *Human Organization* 62 (1): 39–49.

———. 2006. *Janitors, Street Vendors, and Activists: The Lives of Mexican Immigrants in Silicon Valley.* Berkeley: University of California Press.

INDEX

culture
anthropological notions of, 101 n. 6
and "work ethic" of Mexican
immigrants, 82–83

De Genova, Nicholas, 134
Department of Labor, 37
Díaz, Porfirio, 28
documents
fraudulent, 54–55
drug use, 5

economy (U.S.)
effects of undocumented workers
on, 126–128
globalization of, 32–33, 131 (see also
Mexico, economic
globalization and)
and service sector, 34, 37–38, 40
n. 50, 129
and undocumented labor, 32–34,
36–38
ejido, 22
"el enganche", 29
employers. See Mexican immigrants,
supervisors' perceptions of;
undocumented immigrants,
employers' preferences for
employment
of undocumented immigrants,
37–38

families, transnational, 47–49
gendered division of labor in,
120–121

gender, 118–121
globalization, 32–33, 131
effects on Mexican economy, 33–34
and migration, 33–34
Great Depression, 29–30

Hart-Cellar Act, 31–32, 130
hate crimes, 36
Heyman, Josiah, 111

households. See undocumented
immigrants, households of
hispanic
as racial category, 105 (see
also Mexican immigrants,
racialization of)
Hmong refugees, 133
homeless people, 133
humor, 90–92

Il Vino (pseudonymous restaurant),
10, 15–17
Immigration and Customs
Enforcement (ICE), 37
Illegal Immigration Reform and
Immigrant Responsibility Act
of 1996 (IIRAIRA), 35
immigrant rights marches, 36
immigrants, Mexican. See Mexican
immigrants
immigrants, undocumented. See
undocumented immigrants
Immigration Act of 1917, 28
Immigration Act of 1965. See
Hart-Cellar Act
Immigration Reform and Control Act
of 1986 (IRCA), 34, 37
import substitution industrialization
(ISI), 30
International Monetary Fund, 32, 33

labor. See also work
flexibility of, 86, 97, 134
and "opportunity hoarding," 98–99
recruitment of immigrant workers, 25
service, 37–38
undocumented, 37–38
León, Guanajuato, Mexico, 5, 8, 44–47,
60–61
liberal development, 28, 38–39 n. 5

MacLeod, Jay, 116
masculinity, 118
and fathering, 118–120
and ideals of bravery, 99–100